A POUND
OF FLESH

A POUND OF FLESH

Producing Movies in Hollywood—
Perilous Tales From the Trenches

Art Linson

AVON BOOKS ◆ NEW YORK

AVON BOOKS
A division of
The Hearst Corporation
1350 Avenue of the Americas
New York, New York 10019

Copyright © 1993 by Art Linson
Cover art by Paul Stinson
Published by arrangement with Grove/Atlantic, Inc.
Library of Congress Catalog Card Number: 93-22889
ISBN: 0-380-72401-4

The Grove Press edition contains the following Library of Congress Cataloging in Publication Data:

Linson, Art.
  A pound of flesh: perilous tales of how to produce movies in Hollywood/Art Linson.
1. Motion pictures—Production and direction. I. Title.
PN1995.9.P7L485   1993
791.43'0232—dc20   93-22889

First Avon Books Trade Printing: May 1995

AVON TRADEMARK REG. U.S. PAT. OFF. AND IN OTHER COUNTRIES, MARCA REGISTRADA, HECHO EN U.S.A.

Printed in the U.S.A.

OPM 10 9 8 7 6 5 4 3 2 1

To Fi, J and J

Special thanks: Jodie B for tireless re-reads and edits; Barb for always being there; Patti and Colin for assists; Morgan E for his enthusiasm and confidence; Bobby's art; Todd's Macintosh; Miami Mitch, De P, Mighty Bruce, and Fast Rising Tom for generous shoves; and all my friends at Warner Bros. for their indulgence.

CONTENTS

Author's Note   1

Part One: **PREPRODUCTION**   **7**

One: Qualifications
        Finding a Place in the Sun   9

Two: Choosing the Right Idea
        Check Your Pulse   14
        Washing Cars to the Beat   18
        Taser Gunfire at the Beverly Wilshire Hotel   21
        The Milkman Meets Johnny Carson   27

Three: Finding a Writer, Finding Anybody
        Being Nice to Agents   33
        Pick Door Number One   37

CONTENTS

Four: Pitching
         Take Yes for an Answer   40
         He Starts to Go Blind and Doesn't Get Better   46
         Dickens Is Dead   51

Five: Working with the Writer
         Give Me a Wham   55
         Giving Birth to an Opera   65
         Get Him a Chopper   75
         I Invented the Strike Zone   77
         Dosed at the Jerome Bar   84

Part Two: PRODUCTION   89

Six: The Package, the Budget, the Studio
         We Are the Mayonnaise   91
         Blow Me   101
         The Green Light Is Blinking   115
         Musical Chairs   119
         If He Pulls Out a Knife, You Pull Out a Gun   123

Seven: The Cast
         What If He Gets Hit by a Bus?   139
         Are You Talking to Me!   150

Eight: The Director
         The Final Cut   159
         Lost at Sea   165

Part Three: RELEASE   169

Nine: Previews
         Taming of the Shrewd   171

Ten: Opening Night
         It's Not My Fault   186
         It Still Hasn't Gotten Weird Enough for Me   188
         Licking the Icing   193

AUTHOR'S NOTE

This book is for that small and perhaps unfortunate group of people who are thinking about becoming movie producers but do not know how to do it or where to start. It is not for my friends or acquaintances, already living north of Sunset, who have managed to fleece Hollywood and carve out their own maps to the movie stars' homes. It's for the others, with the hope that for their sake it will discourage further competition. Since I have spent a long time doing this thing called "producing movies," I thought the best way to explain "what it is" and "what it isn't" would be to share the many torturous stories that have helped me build the kind of scar tissue necessary to stick around in Hollywood.

This is a how-to book.

Before jumping into the tough stuff, it is important to

isolate that spark which creates the need to be in the movie business, that recessed voice that nags at you, insisting that more upstanding life pursuits are irrelevant, that glamour and money are for you. Imagine being five years old and each Saturday morning your mother dressed you as the Lone Ranger, with a mask and silver bullets, and dropped you off to watch Westerns and comedies at a local theater called the Hitching Post on Hollywood Boulevard. After two years of this, you professed your love for movies and knew deep down that this would be your destiny.

Well, this would be a nice romantic start to this tale, if it were only the truth. Even though I lived at the Knickerbocker Hotel, one block from Hollywood and Vine, the movie theater capital, I preferred television. I'm afraid "The Ed Sullivan Show" hooked me first, not *Citizen Kane*.

Not to say that I didn't like movies, I just don't know when the light bulb went off that said "producing movies is for me."

There was one time.

In 1967 I was a third-year law student at UCLA, married to my first wife, Barbara, and living in a small apartment in Westwood. The Vietnam War was raging, and I was already starting to smoke grass at an old, ramshackle house on Brooks Avenue in Venice, alternating between the comfort and the guilt of avoiding such an awful and incomprehensible conflict. In the midst of this, Barbara and I were invited to a private Hollywood screening at the home of Harold Mirisch by his son, Robert. Robert was also a law student. Our paths had crossed socially. I guess you could call this a Hollywood connection.

At that time, Harold Mirisch was the most prominent producer in Hollywood. Credited with the Academy Award–winning *In the Heat of the Night,* he was rich and esteemed. I was rather unaware of his status as we entered the vast Beverly Hills driveway, but by the time you hit the front door, you didn't have to know how to type to figure out that Harold was not getting paid by the hour. The living room was lavish, filled with food and sprinkled with recognizable faces. It was the first time I had ever seen a screening room in someone's house. It was the first time, for that matter, I had seen Kirk Douglas "live" in anybody's house.

None of this was particularly noteworthy except for the fact that it was also the first time I had ever laid eyes on a real movie producer. How many of you have actually met one? I remember being very curious about what distinguished this guy from the others. There was nothing about Harold that seemed particularly special. Physically, he was on the tiny side, but confident. He mingled well. Dressed with assurance. I guess he was smooth. This was not much to go on, although in time I realized there was a definite pattern at work here.

I even remember asking his son the inevitable question, "What exactly does your dad do when he produces movies?" His eyes drifted to his shoes while he mumbled a few awkward sentences like "He doesn't use his own money," "He gets scripts," "He makes attractive packages," "He schmoozes with stars." Then, after more probing, he quietly said, "Shit, I really don't know what he does, but he happens to be very very good at it." I soon discovered that no one was able to explain exactly what the hell Harold did. But it looked good.

Wanting to be a movie producer was an unseemly ambition in 1967. The Beatles, Bobby Kennedy, Martin Luther King, *Harold Mirisch!* Nonetheless, after sitting through *Guess Who's Coming to Dinner,* listening to the postmovie bashing, and eating what I learned years later was Chasen's Chili, I thought without embarrassment, but with a dose of vanity, that I could do this. I just had to figure out what it was.

In those days there was no book or class to help you break the ice. I muddled through, spending as much time between Sunset and Wilshire and Vermont and Doheny as I could, using the theory of osmosis, hoping that the mechanics of Hollywood would somehow seep in. Seeing movies, meeting people, reading about "the business" was a slow process. I would bang into walls and wait for the scabs to heal. Eventually some of the fog started to lift. I was connecting.

It took seven years after meeting Harold Mirisch for me to produce my first movie for Warner Bros., called *Rafferty and the Gold Dust Twins,* starring Sally Kellerman and Alan Arkin. Before its release, at the first preview screening, one of my guests, who owned Roy's, a Jewish-Chinese restaurant on the Sunset Strip, asked me what I was thinking when I chose to make this sort of a movie.

"What do you mean, what was I thinking?" I asked.

"Well, no one is going to come!" he said.

"How do you know that?" I insisted.

"Couldn't you tell by the story that no one would come?"

"No."

Three weeks later the movie opened to some kindly reviews. I drove to a few theaters in Hollywood and Westwood, with guarded hopes, to stare at the lines. There weren't any lines. He was right. No one came. The movie died ugly on its first weekend. It was a bomb.

I was ice cold before I even had a chance to warm up.

Fortunately for me, people did start to show up for some of the other movies that I produced, but not without much pain and suffering along the way. My guest's restaurant, by the way, is now a rear entrance to a tattoo parlor.

So, in attempting to explain this wobbly journey, I will take you "backstage," behind closed doors to see the machinery hum and spit and to meet the people who are taking the ride. I will begin by answering simple questions, such as "What kind of qualifications do you need for this job?" followed by more serious questions such as "How does one conceive, develop, and package movies?" and ending with more challenging issues like "What happens to you if you don't save your money after making three bombs in a row?"

As you will see, producing movies can often be a bloodstained affair. But, if you can figure it out, it will definitely keep your pool heated.

Part I

PREPRODUCTION

He sees a story, he gets an urge to do it.
—Sam Spiegel

[Part I]

INTRODUCTION

QUALIFICATIONS

FINDING A PLACE IN THE SUN

"Ivan the Terrible with a car phone!"
"Greed untempered by reason!"
"Whore!"
David Mamet was shouting into my car phone after I asked him recently to help me define a movie producer. Now, David and I have done several movies together, for which he was paid most handsomely, so I knew he couldn't be referring to me. Nevertheless, before getting too far into this, you should know that "producers" are not always held in the highest esteem. We are compared to Willy Loman, not Arthur Miller. We flash the accoutrements of power, but rarely achieve it. We

beg for respect, but more often get passed over. Is it because producers have to sell or have to be tenacious or have to always come back for more? It's hard to tell. You can be sure, however, that there will not be a Mt. Rushmore etched into the Hollywood Hills with Harry Cohn's face grandly carved next to Joel *"Die Hard"* Silver's, at least not in our lifetime. This is not meant to start you off on a discouraging note, merely to illustrate the terrain in which you are venturing.

Our ancestors did not help much. Sam Goldwyn started as a top glove *salesman,* not a top glove *designer.* During his day, he was known as much for his butchering of the English language as for the pictures he made. Goldwynisms abounded: "We are dealing in facts, not realities!" "A verbal agreement isn't worth the paper it's written on." "Include me out." These phrases, true or false, simply reconfirmed what everyone already believed—that producers are low-rent pretenders. Sam Spiegel's name became a verb. Forget the fact that he produced *The Bridge on the River Kwai,* to be "spiegeled" meant you were cajoled, conned, and pickpocketed . . . not serenaded.

Instead of *artist* that dicey word *promoter* hangs heavy in the air, and occasionally the epithet "hustling shitheel" echoes across the backlot. What can we expect people to think when we see Julia Phillips, ravaged by time, admit on the Phil Donahue show that she produced several movies smashed on drugs while bound and gagged to the bed in her trailer? That on the set of *The Sting,* she was so gone she could have had her wisdom teeth pulled before breakfast and still returned her calls. Newcomers might conclude that if they merely ate a lot of fresh fruit, they would have the necessary qualifications to produce movies.

Don Simpson, who made millions producing *Beverly Hills Cop* and *Top Gun,* is always complaining. For Don, grabbing most of the money is not enough. He hates producing. He clings feverishly to the notion that he is a "moviemaker," not a financier, not a deal maker. What does he mean by that? He doesn't say "action." He doesn't say "cut." He doesn't write. His acting in *Days of Thunder* was mostly left on the cutting room floor, yet he produced the damn thing. I guess the word *moviemaker* carries more weight. It's got dignity. It conveys creativity.

Ordinarily, when the word *creative* gets tossed around, we get all twitchy. Because, no matter how successful we become, without some respectability, we feel left out. We all want to be thought of as creative producers. Is this a contradiction in terms? Does Robert De Niro have to refer to himself as a creative actor? No. Everyone knows he is.

But if you're willing to look closer, you will realize that there is a bit more to producing movies than good salesmanship. What Don means when he says *moviemaker* and what Don does have—what all good producers have, whether they grasp it or not—is an *instinct for a good idea*. An idea that if properly realized will move, entertain, and hopefully attract an audience. There are no special qualifications necessary to achieve this state of mind. It's visceral. It doesn't matter if you are male or female, educated from an institution or from the street.

What the movie is going to be about and what the movie is going to be based on are often decided by the producer. He must dream it up, have the first concept of what the picture should be when it is finished. Before a word is written, a part cast, a director considered. The most significant contribution a producer makes to a movie occurs months (sometimes years) before the first day of shooting. For better or worse, he is the guy who says, "This is brilliant! If I can only raise a little money and get a script, everybody is going to see this baby."

When you are really doing it right, you are expressing

your personal point of view, your taste. If the movie turns out to be ridiculous and fails, you will eventually get caught and probably make a feeble attempt at becoming an agent. If it works, Don and the rest of us will be the first to say, "Hey, how about a little 'creative' credit? C'mon. I spilled some blood here."

Producers may just be the least understood figures in the industry. Could it be that Mamet is being a little too harsh? I tried to catch him in a calmer state when I could press him further on this issue, believing that his initial response sprang from some unrelated irritability. After all, he had won some awards and could afford to be gracious. We met for lunch. I waited until we finished eating before I repleaded my case. I reviewed the work of some of the more prolific producers in town, providing brief comments on what I thought they had done. He stayed alert.

"Now, don't you believe you were being a little too harsh on the phone?" I asked.

"Well, perhaps you're right," he said. "Art, after listening to your heartfelt explanations about the virtues of movie producing, let me sum up my feelings this way." He paused to throw back the remainder of some strange-smelling tea brewed from a tea bag he had brought to the restaurant. "If you throw a movie producer out of an airplane, he will go *up!*"

There is still no reason to get discouraged. Ideas for movies are plentiful. They can be expensive, like purchasing the new, hot, best-selling book. Or they can be as free as the wind, like dramatizing a news item or historic event. If you can find a writer, a real bona fide screenwriter, and develop a good script based on this notion, actors, directors, agents, and even studio executives will eventually find you. Naturally, this makes writers very important to producers. We have to be nice to them. We have to get to know them. We have to sleep with them. So, even if David Mamet bites the hand that feeds, we come back for more.

If you can't get a window seat at Le Dome for lunch, if you are not Mike Ovitz's exercise instructor, if getting a "drive on" pass through the studio gates seems beyond your reach, even if you are tall, you can still become a player in Hollywood. The instinct to choose the right idea, the ability to find the appropriate writer, and the grit to get your foot in the door are what you need to get started. Here's how it works.

CHOOSING THE RIGHT IDEA

Your father runs a studio or owns a television network or, better yet, he has acquired a vast industrial fortune. He comes to you and says that he always felt you had a strong aptitude for producing. That watching you negotiate for your new BMW convertible was impressive and he wants to help. He provides you with a million-dollar fund to purchase movie properties, rents you a house in Brentwood, and gives you enough change so you can throw the right social and charitable events to bond with the Hollywood power elite. Within six weeks, with your father in attendance, you have breakfast with Katzenberg, lunch with Diller, and dinner with Schwarzenegger. You have bought the latest best-seller and are already meeting with directors to see if they have the right élan. Well, if you're one of these people, you don't need this book. You are already off to a good start in movie producing—it's mortality that might sneak up and get you.

The rest of us, without legacy, have to take a harder look at our options. Everybody at one time or another has said, *"That* would make a terrific movie." Whatever *that* was is the first step in the process. It's the start of an idea. It's basic, it's fundamental, but this is where we have to begin.

A book.
A play.
A song.
A news event.
A magazine article.
A historic event or character.
A personal experience.
A remake of an existing movie.
Any combination of the above.

These are the sources that ideas are derived from. This may seem basic, but it is important to keep in mind that some of these sources were created by someone else, and therefore usually are owned by someone else. If it is a published book, a play, a screenplay, or an article, the author usually has a copyright, which gives him ownership of the use of that material for a maximum of fifty-six years. Simply put: if you want to "copy" from that property, you are going to have to get the owner's permission. Permission costs money. If you're going to develop a screenplay based on a source that is owned by someone else, you will have to buy it or purchase an option to buy it at a future date. If the copyright has lapsed, it is in the public domain and anyone can make use of it for free.

For the beginner, this does not have to seem overwhelming. Except for the hot, new best-seller or the latest standing-room-only play on Broadway, most literary properties are sitting around without attracting much interest. Books that have been out for several years can frequently be optioned at very reasonable prices. For as little as $5,000 or $10,000, you might be able to negotiate an option on a book and hold those rights for a couple of years while you develop a screenplay.

Ideas, news events, historic events, old books that no longer are copyrighted can be free. The next step, of course, is to find a screenwriter to adapt this material. If you can't afford to pay a pricey writer for an adaptation on your own, there are other options available. You can try to convince a studio to finance the screenplay. We will meet those people later on. You might try to find an independent financial partner to support the initial costs of development. You can even ask a writer to join you as a production partner, encouraging him to take less now and more later. I will clarify some of these areas as we get further along.

For now, assume that you can meet the right people and that deals can always be struck. The deal is never the primary consideration. Once you have the correct ingredients put together, the deal will find you.

The first trick—the most important trick—is to find something that gets your heart beating. Other books about Hollywood (and I'm afraid I have had the misfortune of wading through most of them) start to stutter and sweat when they approach this area. Everything can be explained except inspiration. They will give advice on how to find the right story elements: an appealing theme, good conflicts, attractive main characters, a provocative plot. Or you get a tidy lecture on whether to develop a comedy, a social drama, or a love story. The problem is that no one quite understands the mystery of getting movies made, least of all the people trying to explain it in books, if they are to be judged by their general lack of success as film producers.

As we shall see, a good idea to one person is an outrageous embarrassment to another. When I first mentioned my desire to make a movie about "a day in the life of a car wash" put to music, people would stare blankly at their shoes, hoping that I'd leave before some of this cloddish thinking spread. They were certain that I was trying to make my version of *The Gong Show, the Movie.* But no one is standing firmly enough to really know what works.

You can definitely disregard any discussion of what statistics make hits at the box office or what stories attract stars or what kinds of movies fit the studio bosses' taste. This is more nonsense. It is chasing rainbows. I'm sorry. There is nothing to learn. There are no formulas. There is no list. You are trying to find that elusive thing that makes writers and/or studio executives say, "Now that is one motherfucking good idea. How do I get to know you better?" And there are simply no rules in place that exceptions do not disprove each week.

After directing *American Graffiti,* which was a huge hit for Universal Pictures, George Lucas wanted to make *Star Wars.* As legend has it, he pitched the idea of a modern, high-tech version of Buck Rogers to Universal, thinking they would finance most anything after his brilliant success. George, being young, was suckered by another Hollywood axiom that did not pan out; that is, "You are only as good as your last picture." *Graffiti* had gone through the roof. Unbelievably, Universal refused to make his next picture because there was another ridiculous prevailing rule, that science fiction movies were death at the box office. Fortunately, George didn't pay much attention to the platitudes of how-to books, and he got the movie made at Fox. Of course, in the copycat mentality that pervades Hollywood, many sci-fi movies followed *Star Wars,* and most have failed. Popular genres, which are thought to be sure things, do not really exist. Only good execution makes hits.

There is but one standard in choosing an idea, and that is pick the one that excites you. Really excites you. It may sound simple, but it's the only thing that works. When you hear it, you get that little buzz, an itch, something that makes *you* feel that this idea is special. Too many people in Hollywood, most of whose careers are dangling by a thread, spend their hours trying to figure out what will make Jeff Katzenberg, head of Disney, wiggle. It's an impossible task. A bad gamble. Jeff may change his mind. He may not even know what it is he likes until you tell him.

One crusty old producer told me he had only one test when listening to an idea: "Does it make me *laugh,* does it make me *cry,* does it make me *come?*" Excellent. To the point. Your gut is your guide. If you don't think you have a good one, it would be wise to get out now, before you've wasted vast sums of money on subscriptions to *Daily Variety* and the *Hollywood Reporter.* If you think you can stand the abuse, carry on.

The evolution of these ideas can take the most peculiar turns.

WASHING CARS TO THE BEAT

That elusive idea can show up at the oddest time and in the oddest way. You have to be ready to receive it.

In the early seventies, The Troubadour, a club on Santa Monica Boulevard, was the hot music palace that competed with the Whisky a Go Go on the Sunset Strip. Since the music scene had reached its high point, actually eclipsing the movie business as the chic action in town, agents, managers, music producers, writers, actors—I can even recall Candice Bergen standing around the bar—would congregate nightly in front of The Troubadour, trying to get in on the heat. Next door was Tana's, an Italian restaurant that had the good sense to extend charge accounts to the strange-looking people with long hair and untidy dress who were getting thrown out of other establishments—particularly if they were in the music business. They were the new group in town with cash.

Sitting in one of Tana's back booths was Gary Stromberg. We'd been friendly when we were in high school. Both of us had been rather square, card-carrying members of the Huskie golf team, but it had been over ten years since I had seen or talked to Gary. The wonder and drama of the sixties affected everyone, but one didn't need a graduate degree to see that Gary had been severely altered. He was dressed in full African dashiki day wear that would bring pride to any member of the Masai tribe, his long hair was draped over many necklaces, and he was drinking margaritas with Hugh Masekela and three beautiful black girls.

To my shock, Gary, with his partner, Bob Gibson, had become the biggest rock music publicist in Hollywood. His press agentry was touted as young, hip, psychedelic, and deceptively casual. Leftover dried flakes of cocaine would be conspicuously stuck to his mustache. His deliberate use of phrases like "flash lots of flash" or "new is best" was contagious. He knew what it was like to be on the road with Jethro Tull. He was "happening." Apparently, promotion and ideas were his métier.

On this particular night, six months after we got reacquainted, Gary looked like he was trying to calm down from a rattling day.

I had just failed miserably at the box office with my first

movie, *Rafferty and the Gold Dust Twins,* and knowing how long it takes to develop scripts, I was trying to enter the music business to supplement my income. I actually saw Gary and thought, What an unlikely connection, not realizing that he was thinking the same thing about me.

As he came over to my table, Gary pulled a tattered paper napkin from his pocket and placed it in front of me. At the top he had written the words "car wash." Underneath was a bizarre list of what I was told were song titles. Unfortunately, I can't remember all of them, but here is a small dose:

> "Niggers and Jews Have the Rights to the Blues"
> "Brothers"
> "You Gotta Believe"
> "I Used to Hate It till I Ate It"
> "Hog Man"

This last one was going to be a song about a guy who drives a Caddy and washes cars with his body. He lathers up and rolls over them.

Did I say, "What a great idea?"

Yes.

For some odd reason it struck me funny. Life at a car wash. The strange thing about ideas is that, if I had picked up the same napkin three years later, it might have turned me off completely—the right time and the right place and it starts to make sense. We decided to become partners and try to get some money to develop this. Even though I was still laughing, I cautioned Gary that when we brought our little gem to the studios, they might not regard it with the same enthusiasm.

People in the movie business then were traditionally more conservative than those peddling records. I suggested that we come up with a better form to present this idea, that these song titles might scare off someone who'd had a normal childhood, that perhaps we should leave the liquor-stained, tattered cocktail napkin at home. And last, when we finally got our big meeting, for the sake of the project, he should consider a less colorful dashiki.

He agreed.

TASER GUNFIRE AT THE BEVERLY WILSHIRE HOTEL

As the elevator doors opened on the ninth floor of the new wing of the Beverly Wilshire Hotel, I could hear a loud, deep shriek followed by three strange popping sounds coming from the fire exit at the end of the hall. A young floor maid with a slackened jaw rushed passed me carrying some soiled wet towels. Wearing only one shoe, she was limping badly. This exaggerated her distress as she disappeared through a service door.

Three months before, in the spring of 1978, I had read "The Banshee Screams for Buffalo Meat," an article written by Dr. Hunter S. Thompson for *Rolling Stone* magazine. It is hard to say what motivates somebody to choose an idea for a motion picture, but in retrospect I see that choosing this article was simply a diabolical act. I had, like everyone I knew, read *Fear and Loathing in Las Vegas.* The notion that two armed guys, driving to Vegas in a convertible, would douse the car's floor carpeting with ether just to smooth out the journey was comforting to wimps like us who were merely on the lookout for good weed. While they were trying to balance their psychedelic mix, we were wearing the cigarette burns of our generation as badges of honor.

The article was plain enough. It was Hunter's reflection

on a friend, Oscar Zeta Acosta, who'd disappeared under grim and mysterious circumstances in 1975. Oscar was the "300 pound Samoan attorney" who was eating acid in *Fear and Loathing*.

When I read Hunter's lamenting portrait of Oscar—

He was put on the earth for no reason at all except to shit in every nest he could con his way into—but only after robbing them first, and selling the babies to sand-niggers. If that treacherous fist fucker ever comes back to life, he'll wish we'd had the good sense to nail him up on a frozen telephone pole for his thirty-third birthday present.

—I was touched. Now I don't know what kind of condition this puts me in, but I was sufficiently motivated to claim that this was the "buddy" movie of the seventies.

Since I had already learned that Hunter had sold the film rights to *Fear and Loathing in Las Vegas* to several people at the same time—thus muddling any chance of getting that book made—the only movie left to make was some bastardized fictionalized version of this article. The last go-around with the Doctor and the Brown Buffalo. It would be grand mayhem for those of us trying to recover from the assassinations of our leaders and the stench of Nixon's wake. It would be a comedy. Hunter stated in the article that "it was hard to feel anything more than a flash of nervous humor at the sight of some acid-bent lawyer [Oscar] setting fire to a Judge's front yard at four o'clock in the morning."

After some effort I got Hunter to call me back, and I told him of my interest. I mentioned that there might be some money involved. He said to bring him to L.A. as soon as possible, that this was too important a subject to be discussed on the phone, that secrecy should be maintained. Now I wasn't so naive as to think that he was trying to get a free trip to Hollywood just to visit with me, but when a producer gets excited about an idea, strange rationalizations creep into his consciousness. You don't hear the siren when you have an erection.

In any case, after setting up Hunter for the trip to L.A. and charging his hotel room to my American Express card, I arranged a meeting with Ned Tanen, who was head of motion pictures at Universal, and his vice president, Thom Mount, to tell them of my brilliant idea—the modern-day tie-dyed version of *Butch Cassidy and the Sundance Kid.*

Tanen, square jawed and direct, punishes himself daily for the few bad choices he has made and rarely enjoys the many good ones. The doom on his face at meetings only confirms his deep conviction that the chance of getting out alive in the movie business is almost nil. This does not always provide an atmosphere of joy when you start your spiel. Mount, a smooth-talking, waspish North Carolinian, seemed strangely at home in the house that Wasserman and Stein built.

"It's a natural. A cross between *The Wild Bunch* and *Some Like It Hot,*" I said. I knew how to sell.

"Do you have any idea who this guy is?" Tanen howled.

"He's a writer. Writers are my friends," I said.

"I believe he ran with the Hell's Angels," Thom chimed in.

"It's going to be funny," I countered.

"The Hell's Angels!" Tanen echoed.

"He's a great writer, and he wears glasses. How complicated could this get?"

If there is one axiom in Hollywood, it is that people associated with a hit picture get a chance to make another movie, although not necessarily at the same studio. Since no one knows what makes a hit, they figure the best shot they have is to at least give the money to someone who has already done one. For our purposes, it doesn't matter how the rest of

this meeting unfolded, because the last picture that I'd produced for Universal was *Car Wash*. The picture cost $1.8 mil-
lion and made all the money back the first weekend it was
released. It was a hit. Think about it. Was the Thompson idea
any stranger than a movie about the day in the life of a car wash
put to music?

Maybe "weird" would work.

I was carrying a little bit of credibility around the studio
hallways after *Car Wash* was released. It was like having a
savings account. Naturally, I was asked to develop movies
about "a day in the life" of a hamburger stand, a gas station, a
disco, et cetera. But I decided I would have none of that. I had
a plan. I wanted to walk a higher path. I decided to spend all
this newfound cachet on *The Banshee Screams for Buffalo
Meat*.

Why I did this is something I've been trying to figure out
for years. Some called it a characteristic need to self-destruct
from the guilt of winning in Hollywood. I always felt it was
curiosity run amok. Good weed. A victim of my decade. Let's
face it, if you're going to choose an idea for a movie, you may
as well make it something that you are at least interested in,
something that you would go to see. I was still too green to
comprehend how far the drop could be.

"OK. We'll give you some money to bring this guy to L.A.
for talks," Tanen warned, "and a little money to secure some
rights, and even a little money to develop a screenplay. But
Hunter Thompson is your responsibility, Linson. We do not
want to hear about any problems." Tanen, in spite of himself,
always had a hankering for something fresh.

"No late-night phone calls," Mount parroted his boss.

"I won't let you down."

As I walked down the dimly lit hallway to Hunter's room,
I had a simple strategy. If he would sell the rights to fictionalize

this article, we would pay him not only for the article but also as a technical consultant when the movie got made. Ten thousand dollars felt like the right place to start.

"Money. You are going to get money, and you won't have to do anything for it, not even write the screenplay," I rehearsed.

A loud crash of a lamp falling on a hard floor sounded through the door after I knocked. Hunter opened the door and invited me in. He had the same querulous, dazed look that he did in his photos, except that he was much bigger. His size added danger. The first thing I noticed in the room was a gashing four-inch hole in the wall by the side of a picture above the couch. Scattered on the coffee table were some of the books he had written.

"What's with the hole?" I shouted through to the bedroom, where he'd gone to change.

"It was an accident." He reappeared holding a gun. "This new Taser wasn't supposed to carry past fifteen feet."

He walked off seven paces from the wall, turned, and fired. Another gaping hole blasted through the wallpaper.

"Christ, these specifications can't be trusted."

My hand instinctively reached for my wallet, which contained my American Express card. Would the black tower at Universal City accept this damage as an entertainment expense? Tanen was not going to be pleased.

I suggested that we go out to discuss the details of our future deal, thinking any further destruction in a public place would—arguably in a court of law—not be my responsibility. We drove to Roy's, the trendy Chinese restaurant on the strip, where I secured the prized booth perched in the middle of the room with a curtain if one wished for total privacy.

The waitress came by, took our drink order, and closed the curtain. A strange look came over Hunter's face. She returned shortly with several shots of Chivas, three margaritas, Heinekens, and some vodka on the rocks. She gave Hunter a curious look and quickly shut the curtain again. Conversation became uneasy. We were trapped in a cave. He managed to say that he wanted to be paid in cash only. No checks. No check stubs. No records. He kept gazing around the cloistered booth. I could tell that he was in no mood to discuss business. He warned me that Oscar was probably not dead, that he could come back at any time and there could be major, major shit to pay. Once he invoked Oscar Acosta's name, his humor faded. He screamed and flung open the curtain. His fist pounded the table.

"Arggh, I need air! Damn, man, just get me the *money!*"

The curtain had swung back and knocked over my drink. We were both drenched in sweat. The restaurant stopped only briefly to stare at the dazed outburst. I guess my zeal to "close" in the private booth had created an impossible claustrophobia for Hunter. This ham-fisted meeting was clearly not servicing a future friendship, but the process was working. An idea was chosen, a deal was made. The rights to fictionalize the article were sold.

I suggested that Hunter become our technical adviser. He leered at me over his glasses. He could see the endless possibilities this provided for him. I had second thoughts but I felt that having Hunter around would allow me to keep a peripheral eye on him, thus avoiding the inescapable ambush. I was flying on blind instinct now; the more razor edged events became, the more confident I became. After all, I had a cheap hit under my belt.

As you might have assumed, this adventure did not end over Chinese food, nor did it end pretty. As we move into other topics of filmmaking, this saga, later known as *Where the Buffalo Roam,* starring Bill Murray as Dr. Hunter S. Thompson, will resurface.

Or, as Hunter used to say, "The condor is out of the closet."

THE MILKMAN MEETS JOHNNY CARSON

"156 MILLION DOLLAR GOOD DEED" was plastered in a huge headline across the *Los Angeles Times*. Underneath was a photo of Melvin Dummar reading the news with a sheepish grin. The story continued:

> A "good samaritan" deed eight years ago by a 31 year old Utah service station owner may have earned him more than $156 million when he was named as an unexpected beneficiary in the purported last will and testament of late billionaire Howard R. Hughes.
>
> Recalling details of the incident, Dummar said he had been driving in the Nevada desert, "I picked up this guy who I thought was a bum. He had been bleeding from his ear and had been lying by the side of the road, wearing some kind of baggy pants and tennis shoes."
>
> Dummar said he offered to take the man, who he described as tall, skinny with a short, stubby beard and a big scar on the left side of his face, to a hospital, but the traveler refused.
>
> As they drove along, Dummar said, the man told him that he wanted to be driven to the Sands Hotel in Las Vegas.
>
> "I dropped him off behind the Sands. He didn't tell me what happened. He didn't say nothing and wouldn't talk until we got into Las Vegas.
>
> "That's when he told me he was Hughes."
>
> Dummar said the man asked "If I could loan him some money and I think I gave him a quarter."

"Now that is a good story," I say to Don Phillips, as he carefully watches me read. Don had been working for me as a casting director on *Car Wash,* but he wanted a change. Like everyone else in southern California, he thought being a movie producer was the E ticket, and nothing I could say would dampen his convictions. In a weak moment, I suggested that if he could bring me something good to make a movie about, I would work on it with him. Every day for several weeks, Don would fill up the office with one peculiar idea after another. Even though most of these notions were simply twisted, there was nothing I could say or do that would discourage him. Until one day, as easy as pie, he said, "Why don't you just read the damn paper today? This may be something."

By the time we finished celebrating the possibilities of Melvin's story, a true American fairy tale of a little guy being rewarded by the richest man for doing a good deed, new headlines started to appear. "MYSTERY WOMAN SOUGHT IN INQUIRY ON HUGHES' WILL." "WILL IS FORGED." "DREAM OF RICHES TURNS TO NIGHTMARE." It seemed like the bubble was bursting on this story rather quickly. Melvin wittingly or unwittingly seemed to have been part of a scam to forge a handwritten will from Howard Hughes. Many other wills began to surface, and it appeared that Melvin's, like the others, would be quickly disproved. In fact, we started to believe that there was a greater chance that Melvin would be doing time than that he would be buying yachts and dining with his idol, Willie Nelson.

I told Don, as I was packing for a long-planned vacation in France, that if this was a story about a forger or a hustler, it wasn't much of a movie. He agreed. That night Johnny Carson started his monologue:

JOHNNY CARSON
. . . and speaking of Melvin
Dummar. They found his finger-

prints   on   Barbara   Walters'
contract.

ED McMAHON
Heeeeeey ooohhhhh.

I was feeling good about leaving. Melvin was becoming a National Lampoon, a waste of time. But the next morning on the plane, the newspapers caused me to rethink things. Several handwriting experts, without any reason to be partial, claimed that the will was written by Hughes. Of course, there were some experts claiming forgery, but at this stage they were in the minority. Melvin's will was not going away. It looked like it would go to trial.

In Paris, I'd barely had a chance to rifle through my mini-bar when I got my second call in the middle of the night from Don. "Art, I am telling you, this thing is heating up. Hell, Melvin's parents were on 'The Tonight Show.' Before he pumped gas, he was a milkman who made treks to Los Angeles with his first wife to try to win furniture on 'Let's Make a Deal' and money on 'Hollywood Squares.' The first wife, Linda, it seems, was quite a package herself."

"It's a great story if he actually picked up Hughes," I replied. "If he proves to be a liar while we're in the middle of production, then you and I will be hanging around Monty Hall, trying to win a washer and a dryer, and won't that make a few people in Hollywood very happy? Don, I gotta get some sleep."

"Big mistake." He was relentless.

"OK. Here's my credit card number. See if you can find him in Ogden. Tell him to come to the Beverly Wilshire Hotel on me. I promise you, if you can get him in the room, I will return." That, I thought, would keep him quiet.

The same beautiful stewardess who was on my flight to Paris recognized me as I was boarding the return flight to L.A.X.

We shared glances that only people who go to Paris for one night could. It was not exactly what I'd had in mind for a vacation, but Melvin was now ensconced in the Beverly Wilshire with his Mormon lawyer and their respective families, and I was flying home. By this time, Don had me believing that the whole world was trying to buy the movie rights. I was getting nervous. I even suggested that Don try to keep Melvin secluded in his room until I arrived.

For me, the purpose for the meeting was to see firsthand if Melvin was telling the truth. So long as there was a chance his claim was sincere, a movie might be justified. Naturally, if Melvin turned out to be completely full of shit, I was going to lose some time and money, but at least it would be a private execution. The only way for me to see if there was anything worth buying would be to sit with him for a couple of days and hear the whole story.

"It is the fanciest place I ever saw," Melvin later told the *Los Angeles Times*. "We had chilled bottles of champagne that I almost drank, but I didn't because I am a Mormon, and then these guys from Hollywood come and they're all wearing worn-out old blue jeans, looking, I swear, just like bums or something." I thought we were right in step, but Melvin was already seeing through us.

We listened to as much of Melvin's story as he was willing to tell in front of his second wife, Bonnie, and his lawyer. He resembled a chubby Glen Campbell with an easy smile and very direct blue eyes. He told us of his encounter with Hughes: how they drove together for 120 miles, that the man refused to talk about himself, that they mainly discussed Dummar's life, that Melvin thought he was a wino, and that Melvin, to pass the time, sang some of his own songs to him.

Melvin told us that, even if the will someday proved to be real, he didn't expect to see any money in his lifetime. What would he do with the money if he did get it? He'd send his kids to college, buy a ranch, get a larger house, own a western clothing store, or a music shop or a nightclub. He even admitted in front of the present wife, Bonnie, that when he'd picked up Hughes he was on his way to Los Angeles to try to get back with his first wife, Linda. He seemed so honest and direct that I was incredulous. Perhaps he was a bit of a merry dreamer, but this man was certainly not capable of handwriting several pages of a will that was confounding world experts. He was struggling to hold on to his milkman's job. If the will was a sham, I was convinced that Melvin had been duped.

As we got into the second day and started to hear more of Melvin's personal story, the chance to dramatize this became very compelling. I told Melvin that we wanted to make a movie about his life and that we would negotiate for the rights with his lawyer. Melvin was elated. Remember, Howard Hughes was a dead public figure, so any use of his story resided in the public domain. If the Dummars could agree to a reasonable option, then the initial costs for this idea would not be exorbitant.

As it turned out, we were the only ones even interested.

While we were leaving the hotel room, I asked Melvin if he could sing a few bars of the song he sang for Howard. He positioned himself in the hallway next to the elevator door, looking for a good echo. He obliged, his voice dropping to the deeper tones of a singer ready to audition for Ed McMahon's amateur talent show. He spread his arms and let it go:

A dream can become a reality, and this is all you do.
Work hard, have faith and courage, and it will all come
 true.

Yes, you can rise from a beggar into a king,
With hard work, faith and courage, you can conquer
 anything.

I know what you're thinking, but even this did not get me to change my mind. We had chosen the right idea. One year later *Melvin and Howard* was made. It won two Academy Awards—Bo Goldman for best original screenplay and Mary Steenburgen for best supporting actress—as well as the Best Picture Award from the National Film Critics Circle.

FINDING A WRITER, FINDING ANYBODY

BEING NICE TO AGENTS

I know what's running through your mind: Guys washing cars to music. A milkman who forges a will. Acid casualties. Give me a break. I come up with ten ideas better than this when I have a hangover. Spare me the lecture. I've got ideas. I've got brilliant ideas. I need a screenwriter. I need a deal. Who do I call?

Fair enough.

No matter how hard any of us try to escape the fact, agents are the oil that makes Hollywood run. Agents are a special breed. If they all were to quit on Friday, by Monday a whole new crop would be waiting at the studio gates to fill the void.

ART LINSON

Nevertheless, they are fundamental to the process. You can sidestep them on occasion, but eventually you're going to have to smile and be nice. They hold the invitations to the party. If you're looking for a writer, they've got 'em. If you need to meet with a studio executive, they've got 'em. If you want to meet an actress, they know 'em. If you want to get a good table at a restaurant, they own 'em.

So how do you find one of these full-service knights, particularly when you haven't done anything?

If you are a writer or an actor, it is tough enough to get some agent to sample your wares, but at least you have pages or a tape to show. If you are a producer who has never produced anything, then you are just plain doomed. Why should an agent spend the time with you? In fact, since you have yet to produce anything, you are not a producer, and he really doesn't need you. Instead of viewing this as a catch-22 situation—I can only get in if I am already in—understand that you are nothing and use that as a starting point.

If you are from Wichita, this may be the most discouraging chapter of all. How do you go about meeting somebody when you don't know anybody, and the person you're trying to meet doesn't want to meet you? When I say you don't know anybody, I mean just that. Because the slightest "in," the most modest acquaintance, can get the ball rolling.

I am assuming that you do not even have a family doctor who has a patient who knows Bruce Springsteen's publicist.

Or a dentist who has capped Peggy Siegel's teeth.

Or a lawyer who went to high school and remained friends with an accountant who does tax returns for Billy Crystal's brother.

I mean nobody.

At this stage, the customary advice is to find a list of smaller agencies, which you can get from the Writers Guild of

• 34

America, accompanied by a recommendation that you call each one and say that you are seeking to hire a screenwriter. If you're going to use this method, lie and mention to the receptionist (you will be talking to a lot of them) that you're holding on to a shitload of cash, which you are eager to give to anyone who can write three complete sentences in a row. This may work, but it's extremely tedious, laced with rejection, and is probably going to be dodgy at best.

Like it or not, Hollywood is a social town. It is preferable to meet people in some sort of social context rather than through cold canvassing. Just like moving to a new school when you were young, it may take a while to make friends, but, if you want to get into the game, you're going to have to go where agents and executives go. If you ate breakfast at Hugo's, lunch at Le Dome, and dinner at Dominicks each day for one year, it would be absolutely impossible not to meet and get to know somebody who either is an agent or can put you on to one. That's right, without breaking a sweat, you will, at the very least, eventually spill a drink on someone who is in the business. As personally painful—especially for the shy—and costly as this may seem, it will work. Think of it as tuition and hazing combined. In my opinion, if you have a head filled with good ideas, an extended list of Hollywood hangouts is more beneficial than a list of agencies and production companies.

For our purposes, there is no need to go into a lengthy discussion of the nature of agents in Hollywood. They come in all sizes, from the ridiculous to the brilliant. Their underlying confidence comes from knowing that if one of their clients dries up they can always get another one. Many agents, judging from the histrionics of their press clippings, behave as if they intend to take Hollywood with them when they die. In reality, their clients and their power are usually "divvied up" by their fellow agents at the funeral, before the body gets in the ground.

Don't be shocked when you suggest that you want to develop a Henry James novel that is now in the public domain and the agent tells you that movies about trumpet players are DOA. Some agents (not many) have been known to exhibit more wisdom and talent than the writers and directors they represent. Still, don't expect them to behave like the famed H. N. Swanson, a kindly ten percenter, who actually changed the title of F. Scott Fitzgerald's *Trimalchio in West Egg* to *The Great Gatsby.* He was apparently very patient and responsive to writers' and producers' needs. Today agents are young, aggressive, and looking for the kill. Be prepared for rejected calls, social snubs, and back stabbing. These are normal conditions and certainly not limited to the beginner. Agents have to sell. The less you have to offer, the less your call registers on the meter.

Don't make it personal.

Be nice.

You are going to need them.

If you're new to the game, in need of a good writer but with no more to offer than some good ideas that you want to produce, then I would try to be as damn entertaining at meals as one can possibly be, because no one really believes he needs you. Before you get this far, however, you have to be prepared. Understand the merchandise that you are trying to develop. Devote at least a month to reading scripts from cinema bookstores or from agents you have now met or even from friends. Robert Towne's *Chinatown* is required reading and can be purchased easily. It may be the only screenplay that every agent has either read or had read to him. It is state of the art.

Even at a bar, knowing about scripts can lead to constructive conversations. When I started, I read literally hundreds of scripts. Unfortunately, Towne did not write all of them. For the uninitiated, this redefines pain and horror, because most scripts are beyond dreary. Push through. The worse the writing gets the more you begin to know what good writing is when you find it, and the more you will have to say to agents before you get rebuffed.

Bide your time. Notice and take solace in the fact that when agents do need you, their behavior will radically change. After Carrie Fisher decided to leave her agent and sign with C.A.A.—the same kind of agent you have trouble getting to return your calls—her former agent drove to her house and parked in the bushes, unwilling to take no for an answer. For an agent, losing a viable client is tantamount to dismemberment. Unable to gain entry, yet still displaying inexorable zeal, he called her from his car phone every two minutes throughout the night, pleading for an explanation, demanding another chance to prove himself. Occasionally, through the opening of his BMW sunroof, a high-pitched wail could be heard. By four in the morning, Carrie apparently had to call the cops so she could get some sleep.

When you're in demand, this business generates a lot of passion.

PICK DOOR NUMBER ONE

"A day in the life of a car wash put to music, a day in the life of a car wash put to music," Ned Tanen repeated slowly, chewing on each word as he turned to stare out of his floor-to-ceiling twelfth-floor window. He had such a sad look on his face that after sixty seconds of complete silence, I thought he was going to hurl himself through the plate glass, leaving a perfect human outline. I glanced at Gary Stromberg, who was wearing a shirt with a collar for the first time, imploring him not to laugh or do something stupid.

Tanen is not a man who spends a lot of time delighting in

the good news. He expects the worst. My access to him had been acquired after an initial meeting six months earlier about an idea that was now abandoned. When you're starting out, this kind of access is very valuable. You don't need a course in logic to realize that if you waste these pitch meetings on too many bad choices, it becomes harder to get your calls returned. I was very cautious about bringing him *Car Wash,* and from his reaction I assumed that I would be in executive jail for six months.

"This may be one of the worst ideas I have ever heard." Tanen was coming out of his stupor. He looked at both of us again very carefully, spending a little more time on Gary's African bracelets. We were relieved to see that his expression had turned to bemused confusion instead of abject loathing.

"I think we should make it into a movie," he said out of nowhere.

Stromberg, adequately startled, blurted out, "What!" But I gracefully managed to whisper, "That would be great."

As we were leaving, Tanen asked if we knew Joel Shumacher.

Matching the right writer to the right idea is probably one of your most important decisions. Sadly, I simply cannot be of much help here. I'm usually at a loss when the time comes to say, "I think this guy is the best for this." Of course, you do your homework. You read as much as you can of what each candidate has written and hope that a positive shiver will feed through your body when you meet. I also look at the way he or she dresses (a seemingly worthless observation, but I can't help myself) and consider whether I think I can talk to this person for the next year of my life, whether the studio will be willing to hire the guy, whether we will be able to suffer through several lunches together, and so on. The choice is so important that it can be agonizing.

We read lots of scripts, including one written by Joel Shumacher, which was engaging, and we decided to take a meeting with him. After all, what kind of writer would be good for this idea? It was supposed to be funny, it had to make way for some music, and it could not be condescending to the people who were washing cars. In the end, maybe the best writer would be the one who wanted to do it the most.

When Joel came to my house, he was not what I expected. I guess you could say he was flamboyant. Too tall for a writer, wearing a distressed leather jacket (before "distressed" was the fashion) accented by an unusual amount of Mexican jewelry, he glided in.

"I know what you're thinking, but I grew up under the Chiclets sign in New York, and I know how to make this idea great. There is no one, I mean no one, who can do this better than me," he said before he even sat down.

As Joel talked, he reminded me of a helicopter coming in for a landing—scattered, witty, and interesting to watch. As he discussed potential incidents, he seemed to have a genuine affection for the people. There was no condescension. Joel saw the humor of the characters, but he was not going to laugh *at* them. The meeting was rather brief. After he left, Gary and I agreed that we liked him. For me that was, and still is, a major consideration, but the capper, for us, was that we knew Joel was represented by Tanen's wife, Kitty Hawks. Tanen was sure to hire him.

The development stage had started.

PITCHING

> LEVY
> In twenty-five words. Bruce
> Willis sends Julia Roberts to
> the gas chamber. When he finds
> out she's innocent, he has to
> break into prison to save her
> life.
>
> LEVISON
> Do they fuck?
>
> LEVY
> Who?
>
> LEVISON
> Bruce Willis and Julia Rob-
> erts, in act two, do they fuck?

—from *The Player*, written by Michael Tolkin

TAKE YES FOR AN ANSWER

You are still here. You have a steel-plated stomach, and you are already reading the "trades" on a daily basis. Boffo, SRO, Eisner, three pic pak, Geffen are familiar terms you throw out casually at lunch. You've chosen a good idea. You have even managed to find a writer willing to turn it into a screenplay. You have almost everything but the *money*. Well, when you don't have the money, you're going to have to convince people to give you some. You're going to have to get them really excited about this idea and this writer. Everyone knows that investing in movies can be a ghastly waste of cash. Even your dry cleaner has heard the expression "never use your own money." You're going to have to make people believe that this investment will enrich them not only financially but spiritually as well. You're going to have to explain *in a meeting* that what you've got is too momentous to pass up. In short, you will have to "pitch" your idea. Pitching will surely test your mettle.

Again, like everything else in Hollywood, the concept seems simple enough. It's selling. You would assume that those endless summers working for Fuller Brush would be sufficient experience to help you through. They are not. To the beginner, pitching to a studio executive can be terrifying and even dangerous.

How you comport yourself in a meeting can make or break the pitch. Manners and timing are critical. Movie executives are very sensitive; they just are not necessarily sensitive when it comes to your feelings. One friend of mine went in to pitch his wares. He was seated in the executive office with two junior execs waiting for their boss to come out of his private bathroom. As he exited, the juniors made sure to keep their eyes above their boss' belt line. To lend an air of informality, the players gathered around the coffee table. The boss sat and put his feet up; the others sat and put their feet up. In Thailand, showing people the bottom of your feet is very rude, but in Hollywood it means that we're all in this together.

My friend, being a bit of a fashion groupie, was curious. He wanted to know what kind of loafers a guy who'd recently received an annual $750,000 bonus would place on his coffee table. So, he looked. They were all wet and spotted. The boss had apparently peed all over his Armani suede shoes. Perhaps my friend should have realized that his glance lasted a beat too long, because this delay caused the junior execs to look too. An innocent glance, but the boss clocked it, and they made eye contact.

Under other conditions this faux pas might have been dodged more easily, but my friend was too inexperienced to observe the more subtle nuances of the game. For one thing, his meeting was poorly scheduled. Always make an effort to schedule your pitch meeting before 12:30. Between 12:30 and 1:00, executives are usually too hungry and are already thinking about their lunch meeting. The mere fact that their next meeting will take place over a meal means that it is probably more important than your meeting. Even worse, pitching to an executive directly *after* he has eaten can be very sluggish under the best of circumstances. The buying mood has usually passed. The only call after lunch that really gets their attention is the one from "upstairs."

This pitch was at 3:30.

My friend delivered it well; it was of the "one-line" variety. "An evil twin takes on the identity of his successful brother, seduces his wife, insults his friends, loses his job, pillages his possessions, and puts his brother's life in jeopardy. It is an adventure slash comedy."

Not bad. This generally would get some response. At the very least I would expect, "Oh, *The Prince and the Pauper,* of course. Actually, we already have six of those puppies in development now. But it's such an intriguing twist that we'll have to think about it and get back to you soon. There is always room for more of the same. Oh, and before you leave . . . thank you."

If it's late and the execs are a little worn, their responses get a bit obtuse. "Can one twin be black?" or "Do they have to be twins?" or "Would the wife be more sympathetic if it were coitus interruptus?" Nevertheless, getting some response starts the dialogue, and the meeting is under way.

This time, the room was dead. Everyone was still reeling from the errant piss on the shoes. Not even the junior executives had questions. No one wanted the one-line idea amplified. It took the poor bastard thirty seconds to deliver the pitch, twenty seconds of silence, and ten seconds to leave.

If an executive shits on himself (literally or figuratively), try not to notice.

Assuming you enter the room at the right time and everyone is eager to hear your pitch, there are some basic things to consider. The standard commandment is "whatever you do, keep it brief." Think "high concept." Train yourself to explain your ideas in the style and substance of a *TV Guide* listing. In other words, learn to be a blurb, a one-liner kinda guy, a fool. This is nonsense. If Michael Douglas pitches "a scorned lover threatens to kill him and his family if he does not come back to her," he'll walk away with a deal and they'll probably call it *Fatal Attraction*. But who the hell are you? If that's all *you* have to say, they'll tag your toe and send you south of Olympic Boulevard.

Being brief is an axiom created mainly by the people who suffer boring pitches. They are not trying to help you. They are trying to make their lives easier, and you can hardly blame them. Many executive acquaintances of mine claim that spending a day in a small office listening to desperately sweaty tales is like being tied up and whipped in a crowded bar for thirty-six hours. They go berserk. They beg for the story to be brief and painless.

After all, how many times can you hear, "an accountant cross-dresses at work to show sympathy for the opposite sex, and he learns how hard it can be to make new friends." This is brief, but you better add that Robin Williams has agreed to wear the dress and that you are in possession of some compromising pictures of the studio's controller. You need more than a pithy one-line speech with a slick delivery.

When an executive hears a pitch, he or she is listening for a variety of things:

- Will this idea attract a screenwriter?
- Will this idea attract a director?
- Will this idea attract a star?
- Is this going to cost a lot of money to make?
- Is this similar to something that has already been very successful so I can sell it to my superiors? Even though this approach may work for them, it will eventually strip you of your originality. If you hopelessly pigeonhole your thoughts, your ideas become common. It's a bad habit. Executives will not know why, but soon you will be boring them.
- Do I want to be in business with this guy? Because it means that I'm going to have to talk to him a lot. Particularly if you are new in town and without substantial credits, how you behave is all they have to go on. This is like trying to join a club, and it brings all the baggage and discrimination attendant to that process. All you can do here is shower every day, smile, and hope for the best.

Last, the pitch has to be long enough to get the listeners to participate, to contribute to the idea. "My God, this makes me cry . . . Why, Penny Marshall would be just perfect to direct," or "If we can just make a few minor adjustments, this could be very funny." If this happens, it is a very good sign. It simply doesn't have the same impact if you have to suggest why the damn thing works. They want to believe that they figured it out. It makes them feel creative. If they feel creative, you feel creative. They're not going to be fooled by you telling them with agitated excitement that your idea is a cross between the last two hit movies in release. They only buy into that game if *they* say it.

Say this is your pitch: "A brilliant and witty male African-American scientist, sent to South America to find and destroy a giant prehistoric beast that is eating whole villages, meets and falls in love with the beautiful Irish-American daughter of the CEO whose multibillion-dollar company is raping the third world." You never need to add that Danny Glover would be brilliant with Julia Roberts. They know that. You want to expand the idea as carefully as you can until they to leap to their feet and say, "Holy Jesus, this is a cross between *Jaws* and *Guess Who's Coming to Dinner*. How damn timely."

Whatever the execs add to your pitch should be greeted with a great deal of enthusiasm and—if you can muster it—awe, because once they start investing their own juices, you are getting closer to the money.

I was very fortunate when I pitched "A day in the life of a car wash put to music" to Ned Tanen. Because I was so green, I didn't realize what Tanen was actually hearing. I was thinking, If he goes for this, I should roll up my sleeves and bring out the old watches to sell and definitely ask for another appointment in a week.

What Tanen, who was demonstrating good instincts, actually heard was much more than "what a funny but absurd idea." He knew immediately that this was a broad comedy, that it would be inexpensive to make because it would take place in one location, and that the music, if we could get it right, would be a great sales tool. At the time, I was so far down the food chain in Hollywood that he knew he could get me and my rock-promoting partner for free and I would still say thank you. Before I understood what was happening, the green light was in place. We took yes for an answer.

HE STARTS TO GO BLIND AND DOESN'T GET BETTER

No matter how successful you get, the pitching process is never really trusted by producers or writers.

When the overnight mail recently delivered to me *The Way We Live Now,* written by Anthony Trollope, with a brief note from David Mamet, I was not surprised. David occasionally sends me a book to see if I would be interested in getting him a big check for writing the screenplay. It's not that I'm ungrateful for his submissions, but they are not always what I'm looking for. This book was 1,500 pages long. That would have been 3,000 pages had it not been set in the tiny type that you see in motel Bibles. It pressed all the wrong buttons. Re-creating Victorian England is extremely expensive, finding a simple story in all this would be almost impossible, and the codes of social conduct didn't seem to have a big sexual buzz. Being respectful, I waded through about 60 pages before calling him to ask what planet he was on.

"David, even if I understood this book, how would I be able to pitch it to the studio?" I said. "If you haven't noticed, there isn't a big demand for nineteenth-century parlor dramas that only your English teacher can decipher."

"I think it's amusing and would make a good movie," he said.

"In what Cineplex can you imagine this playing?" This was certainly a question the studio would ask of me.

"You are a man with limited taste, but you're the only one

I know in L.A." He was starting to resign himself to the rejection.

"Do me a favor. I have a life, and thanks for sending me the easy ones," I replied.

He called back three weeks later and asked if I had ever read Andrew Potok's book *Ordinary Daylight*. Maybe I would like to develop that into a movie.

I knew that Andrew was a very close friend of Mamet. I had met him several years before at a dinner in Mamet's New York apartment. Andrew was a wonderfully warm and charming man who I noticed had to be aided to the dinner table. I'd had to leave early and didn't give the incident much thought. But I did remember him.

"Dave, what's with all these calls? Are you starting to rummage through your closets? Last week it was some unreadable torture about manners, and now you're pushing old books written by your friends. Is there a problem at home? Does this have something to do with money? Are you trying to remodel your kitchen?"

"Ah . . . well, I am looking at some expensive houses in Boston," he admitted.

"Oh, well, let's just put my name in the sucker-of-the-month club in your Rolodex." I could afford to be smug at the time because I had a picture in production. This always makes a producer a little heady, some may even say annoying.

Mamet's price, by the way, after writing *The Untouchables*—a movie we will painfully discuss later—*The Verdict*, and *Hoffa* was in the seven digits. He has been known to knock off one of these babies in three to four weeks to support his directing habit as well as his need to lecture and write books. So, naturally, I was a bit cautious. Almost suspicious.

"You should read it or, shall I say, have someone read it to you. It would make a helluva movie," he said.

"OK."

"By the way, it's an autobiography," he said.

"So, I like *real* stories," I replied.

"You *do* know, Andrew's blind."

"Well . . . I guess, I'm not that perceptive, but now that I—"

"Read the book and call me," Mamet interrupted.

I am one hundred pages into *Ordinary Daylight,* and my heartbeat starts to double. It is the moving, courageous, and even funny story of a man, Andrew Potok, who begins to lose his sight and rails against his fate. Before he comes to acceptance, he embarks on a series of attempted cures that are breathtakingly dramatic. I went from thinking, "That son of a bitch is using me as a meal ticket" to "I better not let him know I'm excited or else that bastard will either double the price or (even worse) take it to another producer." I finish the book with tears in my eyes, but they are quickly squelched by the panic that occurs when a rapacious producer desperately wants something and fears he won't get it.

The best approach was to lowball this one, hoping Mamet wasn't sure how salable it was. I waited an extra day before I called.

"Well, I finished it," I said evenly.

"Yeah . . . oh . . . what did you think?" Mamet must have been eating fruit. He sounded so slushy I thought it was a ploy.

"It had some nice things about it. . . . It's a toughy all right, . . . but I think I like it." I was oozing cool.

"But do you think you can get the *money?"* he said. The bait was dangling.

"Gosh, Dave, I can give it a try," I said, knowing that for me it was a slam-dunk. I was by now a relatively successful producer under contract to Warner Bros., and this was a brilliant idea for a movie.

You have to understand that David Mamet doesn't share

the high regard for Hollywood that you and I have. In fact, since he now isolates himself in Cambridge, Massachusetts, or in the hills of Vermont, you could even say he has a pinch of contempt for the place. He assumes that if he likes something—really likes something—Hollywood won't. His *agent* doesn't even live in Hollywood. In fact, when a very prominent Hollywood agent got Mamet on the phone after placing an obscene amount of unanswered calls, he asked Mamet, if his local agent died, would he consider signing with his agency? David, without hesitation, replied that if his agent died, and all the other Hollywood agents died, and Mamet was terminally ill, then he would probably get a lawyer in Boston before he would sign the man's agency papers. Mamet then thanked the man for the three hundred calls.

I could sense, from years of being tortured by writers and by David's reticence, that he thought the studios were going to hate this idea, reconfirming his suspicions that the town is terminally asleep.

"OK, let me get this straight. You are going to march into Warner Bros. and say, I want to make a movie about a guy who goes blind and doesn't get better." He sounded almost gleeful.

"Yes."

"Make sure you mention that he doesn't get better." Mamet was sure I was going to get tossed out of the office.

"I will."

"I want you to tell them it does not have some Mickey Mouse Brian Grazer ending." He was on a roll now.

"I promise."

"Believe me, they'll never get it. I just read a screenplay that is a 'go' picture with a big no-talent star, and it starts with an establishing shot—L.A. School, 'every brick oozes abandonment.' Did you hear me? 'Every brick oozes abandonment.'" He was cackling.

"I heard you," I said. I was trying to get off the phone gracefully before I had to repeat the pitch.

"One more time," he said.

Now in unison we repeated the pitch, *"He starts to go blind and he does not get better!"*

Despite Mamet's protestations, the executives at Warner Bros. don't live under a rock. Movies that demonstrate extreme personal courage under the most difficult conditions have a long history of performing well, especially if they're executed by world-class writers and directors. If nothing else, David Mamet is a world-class writer. Warner Bros. was very excited about the possibility of doing this, even after I pitched the ending. A deal was struck.

The footnote to this tale is that ten years before, when Andrew Potok had submitted his autobiography to Warner Bros., it found its way to the coverage department. This department, which exists at all studios, reads submissions, reduces them to brief synopses, then hands over its recommendations. The process allows executives to spend their time on more valuable pursuits than reading. There are three little boxes at the end of these coverages: Highly Recommend, Recommend, Pass. For *Ordinary Daylight*, there was a big X in the Pass box. The book was summarily rejected. When it was resubmitted with David Mamet attached as the writer, the recommendation by an unsuspecting new crop of readers was excellent—a must make.

After the script was completed, Penny Marshall flirted with the idea of directing it. She had recently completed *Big, Awakenings*, and *A League of Their Own*. With this unparalleled record of success, we were all very excited about the possibility of her doing the movie. Penny said, "This could be perfect. First I do a comedy, then I do an affliction movie, then I do a comedy, then I do an affliction movie." Finally, after much reflection, she decided to move on to different themes. Since then, the script has failed to attract the necessary ingredients (e.g., star and/or director) to induce the studio to finance the film. It is still wallowing in packaging purgatory.

DICKENS IS DEAD

I want to pass on another rule that will prove helpful if you intend to maintain good relations in town: don't pitch the same idea to two studios at the same time.

In 1981 I was in the middle of a script meeting with Jeffrey Katzenberg and his assistant at Paramount Pictures. The office had been decorated by the production designer of *American Gigolo.* All white, interrupted only by some black, high-tech, macho chairs and tables. Depending on your taste, it either conveyed neomodern excitement or slick, trendy male hard-on. Jeffrey had just taken the helm from Don Simpson, and he hadn't yet had a chance to redecorate. I must say, the look didn't suit him. To Jeff's credit, we were going over script notes of a Christmas tale loosely based on the old Humphrey Bogart film *We're No Angels.* He had inherited the project, had not put it into development, and did not really like it. Soon it was clear that our approaches to this story were not meshing. I was getting increasingly frustrated with his notes and he with mine. I started talking with my hands, and Jeffrey started talking with his hands. The assistant was silently taking notes.

Suddenly, call it an out-of-body experience, I was floating above the meeting, brushing past the latest fashion in recessed lighting, and I had a clear view of the three of us, particularly Jeff, perched on an oversized couch designed for picking up babes. I'm thinking, What a Christmas movie this would make:

a guy, high-speeding to middle age, lost in the vanity and power of a Hollywood career. His charity abandoned, his innocence lost, thrashing around in an overpriced office that screams pimp. My God, it's a modern-day *Scrooge!* It wasn't necessarily about Jeffrey, it was about all of us.

The meeting continued. Our mouths were all moving, but I could no longer hear what anyone was saying. Admittedly, I hadn't eaten in twenty-four hours, and the overcooked studio coffee was taking its toll. I was sweating uncontrollably.

"Dickens is dead!" I blurted out.

This was so out of context that it managed to attract some very peculiar looks. All I could think of was that Charles Dickens had died over a hundred years ago and *A Christmas Carol* must be in the public domain. The idea was free, and updating it with the venality of a Hollywood backdrop would be extremely funny and telling. I quickly thanked everyone for the development hell notes and drove home.

The next day, while eating lunch at Hampton's with Ned Tanen, who was still running Universal, I pitched my idea, and he liked it. I called my lawyer, Tom Pollack, and told him to call Tanen and start negotiations. Pollack, ever cautious, advised me that since I was in development on another Christmas movie at Paramount, I should at least give them the benefit of hearing the idea. A meeting was quickly set with Katzenberg and Michael Eisner.

My pitches are never brief, and my public speaking skills are well below the national average. For me, getting up and delivering a family toast can be hell, so when I have to deliver an ill-fated idea to a group of executives, it will occasionally make sense; other times it can only be considered a mess. When I walk into an office, I rarely bring notes, but on this day I wish I had. I sat down, and Eisner and Katzenberg nodded for me to begin.

"I want to do a movie about Dickens's *Christmas Carol* but set in the modern day . . . Uh . . . Uh, a you know what I mean . . . a story about a guy like . . . a power-crazed, uh . . ."

I realized that I couldn't say it was about a guy like Jeffrey or Michael. I should have just said me.

". . . like a . . . a studio executive!"

Eisner looked at me, expressionless. No one wanted to jump in.

"You know, sort of like a guy that has lost his . . . morality . . . his generosity . . . but a comedy nonetheless . . . yes, funny, very funny."

Flop sweat.

"Ghosts, lots of ghosts . . . exciting special effects."

This time I went blank and completely forgot the thread of my speech. As I was reddening, realizing that I had no notes, I actually came to a complete halt. Now, no one was talking. Katzenberg smiled, and I took it as a kind gesture of pity.

"Maybe if I start over . . . you know, from the beginning."

"That would be fine." Eisner finally said something.

"A modern-day Ebenezer Scrooge from Hollywood," I said rapidly, "who . . . uh . . . greed . . . sort of lost his way."

Get a grip, Linson.

". . . he became, I guess, a complete asshole . . . who . . ."

Katzenberg stopped smiling.

". . . but then again, not really. . . . Are there any questions?"

They grinned and said no, that they would think about it and call me back. They mercifully led me to the door.

Two days passed. Paramount didn't call. Pollack, at my request, went ahead and made a development deal with Universal. When the word got back to Paramount, Eisner called me at home over the weekend. Irate.

"How can you pitch the same idea to two studios at the same time?" he asked.

"Mike, I'm sorry, but I didn't know there was a rule about that."

"Well, there is."

"But I made a complete fool out of myself. I was flopping around the floor like a squid. How could you want this? I wasn't making any sense."

"Look, let me be clear about this. *Don't ever bring me a good idea again!*"

I have enormous regard for Michael Eisner, so I didn't get smart and ask if I could at least bring him some of my bad ideas. Nonetheless, there is an unwritten protocol in Hollywood, and if you cross it, the climb back up the hill can be steep.

In subsequent chapters, you will hear more about this movie that finally became *Scrooged,* starring Bill Murray, directed by Dick Donner and written by Mitch Glazer and Michael O'Donoghue. Oddly enough, it eventually got made at Paramount, but by then Eisner and Katzenberg were already setting records at Disney.

WORKING WITH THE WRITER

> BEN
> Lou? How's Lipnik's ass smell
> this morning? . . . Yeah? . . .
> Okay, the reason I'm calling, I
> got a writer here, Fink, all
> screwy. Says I'm producing
> that Wallace Beery wrestling
> picture—what'm I, the god-
> damn janitor around here?
>
> —from *Barton Fink* by Joel and Ethan Coen

GIVE ME A WHAM

So far so good. You've found something that moves you. If it's a book, you've purchased the underlying rights. Or if you're a poor but resourceful beginner, you came up with an original idea and it's free. You were clever enough to find a writer who wanted to turn this idea into a screenplay, and you actually finessed a studio into giving you money to pay the screenwriter. And you were smart enough to have a little money left over for yourself in exchange for giving the studio the rights to make and distribute the movie—if it ever gets made. Bookmakers call this *vigorish*. In other words, you have made a deal, a "development" deal. Congratulations.

I find that this is a good time to have a small celebration with a loved one. I recommend a quiet, candlelit dinner at The Ivy, where you can hold hands and share that brief, warm glow of accomplishment with at least a dozen agents and executives who arrive nightly to eat crab cakes. Tenderness should never conflict with a chance for a little self-promotion. Although there is no guarantee that a picture in development will become a reality, the small victories should be attended to, because there will be some very dangerous curves in the road ahead. Believe me, this is not one of those "smell the roses" speeches given to you by some old fart waiting to die. As you get closer to that anticipated start date, you will be traveling at higher altitudes, and the drop is awful.

Think of it.

This writer is about to go off and write your idea. How will he go about it? Does he really have an affinity for the material? Well, if you're as paranoid as I am, you're going to want him to give you some idea of his approach before he destroys the gem that you have graced him with. You are about to have a script meeting—the first of several script meetings—on your way to the final draft. This is a very interesting and important phase of producing, requiring skill and deftness. What are you going to tell this "I don't need you anymore now that I have the deal" know-it-all writer to help him come up with a good screenplay? Does he really need your help anymore? In most cases, emphatically yes.

It starts off gently enough. You meet. This can occur at your office if you have one, your residence, or even a restaurant. But it should never occur on the writer's home turf. First of all, most writers are on the peculiar side; their houses tend to be odd places, scattered with books and empty pizza boxes, not places for a comprehensive discussion of a screenplay. Second, you want to know where you're going to be seated.

I'm not referring to that old method by which the producer sets up his office so that his chair, ever backlit, is always higher than the writer's, but it is important to feel familiar with your surroundings. Comfortable. Because the writer will usually be prepared, your approach to these meetings is very important. I have always felt that when you are giving somebody medicine, it is best done in the doctor's office, and it's best to smile when you ask him to open wide.

You can always tell which writers have read Bill Goldman's *Adventures in the Screen Trade*. They walk into your office, skillfully field the brief, amiable chitchat, then pull out a notebook and pen. They stare expectantly into your eyes. "I'm here to serve, just guide me," the baleful glance implores. This is a trick designed to put you on the defense, and it must be countered. The writer knows you probably can't write a screenplay. In fact, in his heart, he doesn't even think you can write a thank-you note. By saying, "Tell me what to do," he knows that your paralysis is about to set in. He's asking you to fix the problem, but that's not your job. Believe me, he has a hidden agenda.

Your gut is still your leading indicator. Don't be afraid of it. You may not be able to explain clearly what's bothering you, but that instinct of "something doesn't feel right here" should be addressed. After all, it's your idea. Articulation helps, but it is not essential. I have sat in many meetings where an executive or a producer, right out of one of those colleges, would sound real smart, but what he was saying just wasn't important. It wasn't from the heart. It was a mechanical approach from a bad handbook. Rhetoric. It became more important to sound impressive than to help the script get better.

This usually manifests itself in the "three-act talk," which seems to be a language everyone but me understands.

"The third act needs to be goosed."

"Make the first act funnier."

"The second act is too long."

David Mamet, in attempting to explain the three-act theory, said that he read a news headline in the *New York Post* which declared, BOY CUTS OFF FATHER'S HEAD, CUTS OFF PARAKEET'S HEAD, THEN CUTS OFF LIZARD'S HEAD. He said the secret is to tell the screenwriter to cut the father's head off last.

From my perch, writers tend to love these suggestions because they don't mean anything. They scribble down "goose" or "funny" or "arc" and say, "Yeah, I got it." They smile sweetly and agree. Sometimes they even thank you. When this happens, you know you have strayed. Because none of this makes sense, they can do whatever suits them.

I say, lead with your chin.

"Remember when you told me that Mary was going to leave her son and get on the bus?"

"Yes," as he writes "bus" in his notebook.

"Well, I almost had tears in my eyes, remember?"

"OK."

"Well, when I read these pages, I felt nothing. Help!"

The only thing he can jot down now is "help."

If it doesn't move you, it doesn't move you. It is your task to tell him. It is the writer's responsibility to figure out why. I've found that the more specifically you can state your emotional responses to the material, the easier it is for the writer to locate the confusions. If your instincts are good, you can be very valuable to a writer. If they're not, it's best to get out of the way, because no three-act blather is going to bail you out. Writers will simply label you a script killer for not being specific enough with your comments. Don't be daunted, writers' guns are loaded with blanks. It's the studio and yourself that you eventually have to please.

As you start down the road with a writer, things can get

really strange. Most screenwriters, after they take these initial meetings to discuss story and tone, want to go off and write the damn thing without further interruption. Few want to discuss what they're doing during the process, and even fewer want to show you pages before they have finished a first draft. With the less experienced screenwriter, this can be a disaster. No matter how much lip service is paid to "let me get it on paper and we can change it later," the ability to do this is rare. All of you who wrote letters to your mother from summer camp, or wrote essays for an English class, or sent memos to your boss know that writing is tough. Each page is a pound of flesh. So when a writer finally turns in his pages, he does not want to throw them out and start again.

He can't help himself, he comes to defend. His face gets all twisted and weird. The body language, as he awaits your comments, is comically stiff. He has been alone in his room for weeks, trying to cook up something special that will further his career. Presumably he has worked very hard, and you—a person with no fucking credit as far as he is concerned—are about to savage his baby with your god-awful thoughts.

When the writer asks, "How do you like the pages?" he is usually barely audible because the words are hissed through a clenched jaw and lips that can barely move.

One of the difficulties of screenwriting is that a screenplay is a very concise form. A final draft is only 110 to 130 pages, loosely typed. Unlike in a novel, there has to be a very direct line of storytelling. The scary part for a producer is that if the writer starts off in the wrong direction in the first 20 to 30 pages, the probability is that the whole screenplay will go south. The wrong story will be told. Imagine having to tell some writer that he virtually has to start over. Had you known what he was doing, you might have saved him some agony.

Under these circumstances, hatred gets redefined.

Let's face it, we are easy targets. Critics without creden-
tials. While you're reading this, I am certain that there are
screenwriters at the Farmer's Market near the espresso stand,
and one of them is screaming, "That piece of shit called me four
times this week just to ask me if it's any good!"

"We know that call!" the other writers shout.

"Of course I said, 'It's fucking brilliant. I get hard every
time I hold it. My wife read it last night in bed and got wet on
every page.' "

"That's the wrong approach," another writer chimes in.
"Those jerk-off producers don't want good news. Bad news
keeps them on their toes. After the second dumb call, I begin
to stutter. I say I've gone blank, that I have been getting dizzy
spells, that I think we're doomed."

"Really, what does he do then?"

"He comes right over with chicken soup," he says as the
others shake and howl.

This little Southland play is performed daily by members
of the Writers Guild at coffee spots all over Los Angeles. The
vitriol has not been exaggerated.

Producers can have twenty-five to seventy-five screenplays in development at one time. The good news is that they
are not dependent on any one script to work in order to stay
active. The bad news is they have to talk on the phone to
twenty-five to seventy-five writers—a daunting and awful task.
Writers are not all a barrel of laughs. Because I don't develop
more than two or three scripts at any one time, each project is
extremely important to me. If they don't work, I'm out of
business. I have no choice. I have to expect that each script in
development will be made.

I guess this makes me a little more desperate than the
others. I make those producer calls—the calls that Bill Goldman warns writers against—while the writer is working if I feel
it's necessary. Now, my calls are not intended to say hello or

check on someone's health. Nor are they trying to find out what page the writer is on. No matter how detailed early conversations about the script have been, there are always a couple of areas that are never truly worked out. Often you start with one or two excellent and original characters thrust into an interesting situation, but the story may not be completely solved. Or the story can be involving but there is the nagging feeling that we've seen this already, that it's not new. Whatever the weaknesses are, it is important that the writer not lose sight of them. Since all aspects of a script cannot be worked out ahead of time, the best stuff can and should be created by the writer when he is writing. Yet a reminder that a structural problem has yet to be solved, and *needs* to be solved, may help. Your intuition will let you know if he is crashing on the rocks.

I recall a situation when I had hired a writer with Paramount's money to develop an original idea (not based on any underlying material) that the two of us had talked out at my house over several lunches. I felt that although everything had not been worked out, it would be a good time for Chris to start writing.

A month had passed since he began, and those dark doubts that he was not addressing all the problems crept into my mind. I made that dreaded call.

"Hello."

"Hey, Chris, *cómo está, amigo?*"

Silence.

"It's Art . . ."

Silence.

". . . Linson."

"Oh."

"Nice day to write. . . . No sports on TV . . . heh, heh," I said, offering my version of small talk.

"Yeah."

"Is there any reason we should meet again to discuss this story? Or do you think we have everything worked out?"

"I'm on it," he said.

What the hell does "on it" mean? It lacked confidence to me. Was I overreacting?

"Does it concern you at all that our climax occurs without knowing why David would be motivated to go back and risk his life for people he hardly knows?"

"No," he said.

That was all, no.

"Oh," I said. Now I'm saying oh.

"Do you think that our choice to use Japanese businessmen as villains is a bit clichéd? After all, it's already becoming a bad joke on television sitcoms."

"This script is the best thing I've ever done," he stated with undeterred confidence.

Had he started with this line, I might have been able to control my paranoia, but to zing it in now meant that things were very shaky. To make matters worse, he then said, "It's writing itself."

It's writing itself!

Now *that's* a chilling response.

Screenplay by Toshiba.

A very bad sign.

He was denying the horror. I asked if I could see the pages before he finished, just to make sure that he was off to the start both of us were hoping for. He felt that this would confuse him and slow him down. He wanted me to experience his whole vision in one blast.

The same dialogue continued off and on for months and months. I nudged, and he reassured. I was trusting that if I raised the tough structural and motivational issues that were still unresolved, he would address them even if he wasn't willing to discuss them. I sensed that he was flailing, but he kept insisting that he was right on target, that there was no reason to look at pages until the draft was complete.

Finally, he called and asked to meet. He said he'd broken the back of it. He was flushed, ecstatic, and ready to go over pages. I didn't know how to feel. It's a bit schizophrenic to be both a cynic and a blind optimist, but when I saw Chris holding a large, black cardboard box, the kind you get at the stationery store that contain a ream of typewriter paper, I believed he had licked it. He set the box on the table between us, just out of my reach.

"It's not quite finished, but if you and I can spend a little time on this, I can be done in ten days or less."

"Very encouraging. There was a time when I thought you might be floundering," I said.

"I have the story perfectly worked out in my head," he said, as he pushed the box over to me.

"In your head," I said distractedly, as I reached for the box.

"It's gonna be great," he said.

"I always knew that we were going to get there," I said as I removed the lid.

There were twelve pages. The box was virtually empty. My mouth dropped.

"Don't be alarmed. I think I'm off to a very good start, and if we can meet every morning and talk about it, I can knock off ten pages a day in the afternoon and we can be finished in a week and a half."

Now he wanted to talk.

I rushed to the bathroom to regroup.

When I returned, he saw the washed-out horror in my eyes. I think he thought I went to get a gun. He reflexively reached for his pages and started to leave. It was clear to both of us that the time for story conferences had passed. It was one of the few times that I was unable to continue with a project.

Tolerance is always an underrated commodity during the development phase.

When you've run out of theories and you can sense that the writer's eyes are getting glassy, you can always pull out the "Whammo Chart." Supposedly Joel Silver got this from Larry Gordon, who got it from some Egyptian who worked at American International Pictures (AIP) many years ago. As the legend spreads, it is a scientifically tested theory that requires each action script to have a "Whammy" every ten pages. This would be a big-action set piece, something that would kick you in the groin and wake you up. If the script wavers a bit, spending a little too much time on nuance and character, it violates the theory. According to the natural laws of physics, without a bang the audience is buying popcorn by the twelfth page and looking for the exit signs if you stretch it to page twenty-five.

So the script gets tested against the Whammo Chart, and the script meeting goes like this: "Go back to your laptop and don't come back until something explodes every ten pages. Come on, give me a wham." I am starting to notice this theory even creeping into comedy scripts.

Silver and Gordon live very well, even if the resultant movies are not necessarily regarded as national treasures. No one seems to know what happened to the Egyptian.

Writing is tough. It can bring out the bitterness in the most gentle person. Again, I asked Mamet how he perceives Hollywood's producers as they approach a writer and his work. Does he feel helped by the process or exploited? I suppose I just like to hear bad news.

Mamet said producers in Hollywood remind him of a cartoon where three vultures were perched on the carcass of a fat hippopotamus. One vulture said, "This is great. A dead hippo, the sun is out, and all our friends will be coming to visit." The other vulture said, "It's like a perfect day." The third vulture started to drool.

Putting all jokes aside, however, producers have every reason to feel anxious. Most writers, if they get off in the wrong direction, simply cannot turn the script around, and the project usually ends up expensively buried in the drawer. In the end, the only thing that matters is that the script is good enough to attract a cast, a director, and the money to get it made. Whatever approach you use to get it there, no matter how embarrassing, I believe is fair game.

It's your job.

GIVING BIRTH TO AN OPERA

I am trying to figure out what lesson one could learn from reviewing my journey with David Mamet as he was hired to write *The Untouchables*. Just remembering it has caused me such anxiety that the only conclusion I can draw is that it has taught me the need for patience, humility—some might say groveling—and, in the end, improvisation. It has also taught me to use the expression "I don't care, you are bought and paid for."

As I was driving down Seventh Avenue toward the Chelsea district in Manhattan, I was considering how to persuade Mamet to write *The Untouchables* for Paramount Pictures. I was never a big fan of the television series, but I loved the subject matter. Al Capone, Eliot Ness, bootlegging, machine-gun violence, and Chicago in the 1930s were a significant part of American folklore. I knew that if we could take the high road, the movie could be great. I wanted a high-priced writer who would distinguish the movie, rather than approach it as another trashy remake chasing a famous title.

Ned Tanen and Dawn Steel offered no resistance.

At the time, Dawn was the most powerful female movie executive in Hollywood, but she did report to Tanen. She was volatile, ambitious, supportive and had long, thick hair. Mamet, who had established himself as a major playwright with *American Buffalo* and *Glengarry Glen Ross* (for which he won the Pulitzer Prize) and as a major screenwriter with his adaptation of *The Verdict,* was at the top of our list. He and I had yet to meet, but I knew he was from Chicago, Al Capone's stomping ground.

When he climbed into my limo, he reminded me of a Jew with a buzz cut trying to impersonate a biker. Judging from his play *Speed-the-Plow,* which he later wrote about Hollywood, I must have reminded him of a clammy rag salesman in casual clothes. I immediately liked him. He, however, remained suspicious.

We went to a small Italian restaurant in SoHo. I waited until we were seated to discuss the inevitable. I thought that the best approach would be to mention the historical significance of the project, to emphasize the intrinsic value in portraying American icons in a meaningful context. It would be a chance for him to recreate his hometown in a legendary way. My head was overtaxed with facts about Al and Eliot. I had committed to memory laborious details of all the plays and scripts Mamet had written, trying to find some connections that would coax him into taking on this assignment.

I was prepared.

The waiter inquired if we wanted anything to drink. I ordered a bottle of wine. I stared at Mamet for a pregnant moment, grinning. Overloaded with so much information, I didn't know where to begin. Mamet just looked at me curiously. I didn't realize it at the time, but the concept of Hollywood coming to visit him always gave him a twisted thrill. It was time to say something.

"Dave, don't you think that the best career move for somebody who just won the Pulitzer Prize would be to adapt an old television series like *The Untouchables* for a *shitload* of money?" I asked. This was the best I could come up with.

Without a beat, he said, "Yes, I think so."

I said, "Great, let's eat."

That was it.

Within four weeks after the deal was closed, Mamet turned in his first draft. Some writers take four months, and many can take up to a year to hand in a draft. This was quick. My cynicism was kindled. Was he taking the money and running, or was he just flat-out fast?

When I read it, I did have some initial concerns: Capone seemed sparsely drawn, and the plot contained some confusions, but the basic elements that made the movie special were all there. The brilliant invention of the Malone character (Sean Connery) as the reluctant teacher of Ness, who helps to clean up Chicago and dies for it, was breathtaking.

> MALONE
> You want to get Capone? Here's
> how you get him: he pulls a
> knife, you pull a gun; he sends
> one of yours to the hospital,
> you send one of his to the
> morgue.

When Capone was finally put away for income tax evasion and bootlegging, Mamet's true-blue, straight-talking Ness provided the only irony in the movie.

REPORTER
They say they're going to repeal
Prohibition. What will you do
then?

NESS
I think I'll have a drink.

For me the screenplay was emotional, witty, and filled with unexpected, memorable exchanges that would distinguish it from the television series. But I felt that there was still work to be done. Two problems, however, had to be confronted: David hated to do rewrites (particularly if they took more than two days), and the studio didn't warm to this first draft, especially after it had been sneaked to a couple of A-list directors who turned it down.

This is how the process works. A screenplay is turned in to the studio, and it is read not only by the heads of the Motion Picture Department (in this case Tanen and Steel) but also by the rest of the staff, which can include as many as ten junior executives. Of course, some of them have more say than others, but in their weekly staff meetings a comprehensive discussion of the merits of new submissions will occur. Those at the top can be influenced by the junior executives, because knowing "what is good" is disturbingly subjective. Needless to say, trying to please a dozen people—many of whom are so inexperienced that they've never been involved in the making of a movie—with an unconventional screenplay can be a very formidable and troublesome affair.

To compound the difficulty, Mamet's screenwriting style is quite different from that of others. Executives, who claim to read dozens of scripts each week, get used to a particular format. Screenwriters learn to write screenplays by reading other screenplays. I assume that when you are confronted with something different, the natural instinct is to think it's wrong. You know, sort of like the white baby chicks pecking out the eyes of the black chick for being different. The first thing you notice about a Mamet script is that the characters do not always sound conversational in the way we are used to. I call it Mamet-ese, and, believe me, it has turned off more than a few executives.

When the mother of the little girl who gets blown up at the beginning of the script visits Ness, she says:

```
                MRS. BLACKMER
It  was  my  little  girl  they
killed with that bomb.

(Beat.)
You see, because I know that you
have children, too. And this is
real  to  you.  That  these  men
cause us tragedy.

(Beat. She nods.)
I  know you will put a stop to
them.

(She nods again.)
And now you do that, now.
```

Is it poetry or is it awkward? Will audiences respond to it, or will they think it's stilted? Will the goody-goody approach to justice be laughed at, or will it be considered a fable? These are some of the questions that ran through the execs' minds, but after getting a couple of director rejections, their first instinct was to retreat and to change the script. There was even talk of getting a new writer and starting all over.

Mamet did one brief set of revisions when he came to L.A. He sat down at the typewriter in my secretary's office and wrote the baseball bat scene:

```
              CAPONE
A man. A man stands alone at the
plate. This is the time for
what? For individual achieve-
ment. There he stands alone.
But in the field, what? Part of
a team. Looks, throws, catches,
hustles, part of one big team.
He bats himself the livelong
day, Babe Ruth, Ty Cobb, and
so on: if his team don't field
. . . you follow me? What is he?
No one. Sunny day, the stands
are fulla fans. What does he
have to say? I'm going out
there for myself. But I get
nowhere unless the team wins!
```

Capone proceeds to bash in the fat man's head.

Even with this scene, Tanen and Steel were getting a lot of resistance from their staff. Feelings about the script were still very mixed. When I tried to get Mamet to do more work based on executive notes, he howled. He said he weighed them before he threw them away.

Tanen even went so far as to say, "Linson, if one person tells you that you are wrong, maybe you aren't, but when they start to line up and take numbers, like they're at Baskin-Robbins, just to tell you a script doesn't work, then maybe you should listen." My only response was, "I have seen those peo-

ple at Baskin-Robbins. Maybe you should send them home."
Things were getting fragile.

If the next director couldn't make sense of this, the new
version of *The Untouchables* would be headed toward the
warmth and comfort of familiar mediocrity. Written by committee and certainly without Mamet.

Brian De Palma, the next batter up, committed.

I will go into greater detail later about the influence that
additional elements have on the studio as you get closer to
production, but, for now, suffice it to say that the inclusion of
De Palma took the studio's executives off the script. Now they
had a "package." Particularly after the expensive *Scarface,* they
started to focus on and fret over the cost of production. Brian
and I wanted some script changes, but we were both savvy
enough to try to collaborate with Mamet on our own. I was
expecting this next phase to be interesting. Neither of these
guys had a reputation as a doormat.

Mamet, being a playwright, is used to retaining enormous
power over the execution of his work. He has been known to
sit in the back of a rehearsal and close his eyes, not even look
at the actors, just so he could listen to the cadence of the
dialogue. Each pause, each stutter he would account for. Not
a line or a word could be changed without Mamet's consent.
He could revel in its sound. He was in complete control.

Well, movies are not plays.

Screenwriters will tell you that the control shifts to the
director once he is on board. This ain't Broadway. You can
either serve the director or face some interesting mental cruelty
as your work gets rearranged. Of course, another option for the
writer is to walk, to wish everyone well and ask to be invited
to the cast and crew party. Rarely is this option considered.

The initial meeting between the three of us, at the Sherry
Netherland Hotel in New York, was like a diplomacy gathering

between Arabs and Jews. Testosterone was spilling onto the rug. We just didn't know how to get started.

"So, how was the cab ride to the hotel?" I said to Mamet. How was that for inane small talk?

De Palma would have none of it. Before Mamet could even respond, he opened the script and said, "David, there were a lot of plot points that simply do not make sense." De Palma was never much of a diplomat, and small talk is beyond him.

"Uh huh." Mamet glanced at me as if to say, "Why don't I just bend over and be done with it?"

"We are here because we think the script is great" is the line I like to start with, but it was too late for that. Swords were drawn. David quickly saw that he wasn't going to be sitting behind the camera with his eyes closed on this one. For him, this was not going to be some great religious experience.

The fact is that De Palma and I had some legitimate concerns. Capone, at this stage, was in only three scenes. We wanted to be able to build up the cameo role, if for no other reason than to get a big actor to commit to it. With regard to the technical aspects of the plot, there were some confusions over the discovery of the income tax evasion evidence as it related to the accountant, and the relationship between Capone and Nitti was very vague. Brian also felt some of the climactic moments could be staged in more dramatic settings, adding a more powerful visual interpretation of the script.

Before David excused himself from the meeting, the only thing he said was that he thought the room service at the Sherry could be improved.

One week later, we received the next draft. It was the last set of revisions that David owed us under his deal. If we needed him for more work, we would have to pay him more money. The plot problems for Brian, however, remained. The good news was that David had added more Capone. The work was sterling. Here's just a taste:

```
            CAPONE
AM I ALONE IN THE WORLD . . . ? DID
I ASK YOU WHAT YOU'RE TRYING TO
DO . . . ?

            OVERCOAT
No, Al, I—

(Capone goes up to Overcoat and
hits him in the face. Pause.
He's    bleeding    profusely.
Beat.)

            CAPONE
(Beat; calm.)
I want you to get this fuck
where he breathes, I want you
to find this nancy-boy. Eliot
Ness. I want him dead. I want
his family dead. I want his
house burnt to the ground. I
want to go there in the mid-
dle of the night and piss on
his ashes.
```

Well, this kind of stuff gives producers wet dreams. I asked David why the rewrite took an entire week, and he told me that it got delayed in typing.

As Brian and I got deeper into other phases of production (some of which will be discussed later), we tried to go back for a third set of revisions. David was being difficult, and who could blame him? The studio was reluctant to give him any more money, and Mamet was about to start directing his own movie. Every time I would call, beseeching his help, he would politely wish me lots of luck with the movie. By this time we were well settled in Chicago, it was four weeks before shooting, and we desperately needed some work done that only David could do.

The problem with rewriting Mamet's scripts is that no one can match his dialogue. It has a different rhythm, a different feel to it. When Brian and I tried to fix some of the problems ourselves, it just never sounded like it was from the same script. Nevertheless, there were two specific things to be done: We needed a scene that tied Capone to the murder of Malone (Connery), and we needed a more exciting climactic scene to catch the accountant. We needed them now.

"Mamet, I need your help," I said on the phone to Seattle, where he was shooting *House of Games.*

"Art who?" was his response, but I could tell he was warming to my call.

"Look, we are up against it. If I come to Seattle, you could do this rewrite in one hour."

"Come to Seattle. I'd love to see ya," he said.

Upon arriving at the airport, I was driven directly to the set. I approached Mamet during his lunch break. He had a new look in his eye. It was the look that most directors get when they are in the full bloom of exercising total control. He smugly pointed out his producer, who was doubling as the still photographer.

"See, this guy knows how to make himself useful," he said.

I suggested that we go where there was a typewriter.

"Why?" he asked.

"Why!" I said. This was getting uglier than even I could have realized. I told the driver to start the car and get ready to go back to the airport.

"All I said is that I would love to see you. I meant it. By the way, where did you get that jacket?" he asked.

"Armani."

"Nice."

"Do you have any suggestions?" I asked, thinking that maybe I should drop to my knees and beg.

"Yeah, tell that greasy bastard that if he gets into trouble, to use that scene from *Carrie* where the hand comes out of the coffin and grabs Ness by the throat."

Back in Chicago, De Palma came up with the "Potemkin steps" scene to dramatize the railroad station, and then we discussed using an opera sequence whereby Nitti could tell Capone about Malone's death. In looking back, I still think our solutions were quite ingenious. Neither scene required dialogue. In the opera, when Nitti whispers into Al's ear, the words are drowned out by the clown's aria, but Bob De Niro's priceless expression tells us everything. Capone ordered and took relish in the murder. We narrowly escaped having to match Mamet's poetic but very idiosyncratic cadence.

When Mamet first saw the opera sequence at an early screening, he was caught by surprise. As he instinctively started to sink in his chair, I turned and whispered, "Be a good sport, you are bought and paid for."

GET HIM A CHOPPER

The few writers—the very select few—who can regroup when the going gets tough are the best screenwriters in Hollywood. They give producers hope.

It was an extremely hot and smoggy day in the valley, and Bo Goldman, the gifted screenwriter who had already won an Academy Award for *One Flew over the Cuckoo's Nest*, was late for his meeting at Universal with Ned Tanen, Don Phillips, and me. We were hoping to get him to write the saga of Melvin Dummar, the milkman who helped Howard Hughes in the desert and was purportedly left a vast sum in a will. We were anxious. Bo was a hot writer.

Bo finally arrived, perspiring, looking like the balding college professor we all wanted. He apologized, said he lived in Malibu and the traffic was horrible. Tanen, scarred from years of attending bad previews, was not known for remarkable patience and did not love to be kept waiting. Now he was listening to Bo as if Bo were telling us a sad tale born from a lifetime of persecution rather than some small talk about sweaty traffic jams. Adding to my surprise, Tanen said, "Gee, Bo, you should have called. We might have been able to get a helicopter to bring you directly." What! I was still having trouble getting a drive-on pass. Tanen, ever astute, keenly knew the importance of a good writer and the disposability of a good producer. He also knew how to close, and he did. Bo Goldman was going to dramatize our idea. I was naturally elated.

After Bo had done extensive research on Dummar and Hughes, he turned in the first draft, which he called *Sonny*. (Sonny is what Hughes's mother called him.) The screenplay, like most of what Bo does, was beautifully written, but the story that was originally discussed had been changed dramatically. The emphasis was on Hughes's childhood. Melvin had all but been written out. It was good, but not the movie we were expecting. We decided to see if we could attract a director and then continue the development process.

Translated: Universal decided to spend more money.

This decision should make a producer giddy. Getting the studio to add an element means you are getting one step closer to hearing the word *action*. It makes sense that the more one can encourage the studio to spend in the preproduction phase, the greater the chance they will stay committed to making the movie. Plus, if we could snag a director now, we wouldn't have to get one later.

The draft was sent to Mike Nichols. He loved the writing, but he was also very intrigued by Melvin's story. He agreed to work with Bo. For the next eight weeks, under Mike's direction, Bo wrote *Melvin and Howard.* It was virtually a page-one rewrite, a completely new screenplay, and it was wonderful. As fate would have it, after months of deliberation, Mike chose not to direct the film. It wasn't the first script that Nichols had walked away from after making it better. He was having a great deal of trouble pulling the trigger in those days; the pressure of failure was overtaking the joy of success. The rest of us involved in the film were exhausted from waiting.

I always felt that Mike made a mistake here, particularly because so much of what was good about the screenplay was a result of his efforts with Bo. Universal stayed committed to making it, however, partly because they had invested so much time and money in development. We then gave the script to Jonathan Demme, who was virtually unknown at the time, and the movie was made. At the Academy Awards ceremony, after receiving his second Oscar for writing *Melvin and Howard,* Bo not only thanked the traditional group of names but also graciously thanked Mike Nichols for guiding him through that rewrite.

I INVENTED THE STRIKE ZONE

The producer doesn't always know what the studio and the young executives are looking for in a finished script, but it is a damn certainty that he has a better idea than the screenwriter.

When it comes to making changes, not all writers come to your office pen in hand, throw a little sand on the floor, and start to shuffle. Once those golden thoughts are reduced to script form, getting additional work without compensation can turn odious. It has been my experience that the first read by the execs is the best one you're going to get. They are not noted for being patient visionaries who bypass the flaws of a script and only extol its virtues. No one enjoys reading screenplays the second and third time. If a script needs work, it is best to get it done before they get their hands on it or it often gets put in *development hell.*

All veteran screenwriters will tell you that this abyss is almost impossible to climb out of. If there are confusions in the material, you get notes. Notes from readers. Notes from junior executives. Notes from senior executives. Notes from agents. Even notes from their wives. Now these notes are combined into one tidy package, presumably intended to fool the writer and the producer into thinking they present thoughts from one giant, great mind. But the jumbled mess of ideas often puts the whole process into a tailspin. Too many chefs begin to taste the food.

In the early 1980s, I began working with Michael O'Donoghue and his partner, Mitch Glazer, both very promising writers. They came up with a wonderful idea for a comedy adventure called *Arrive Alive* about a seedy, incorrigible hotel detective, Mickey Crews, who was trying to bed a gorgeous, tall model, Joy, while secretly working on a series of scams. Set in Miami's colorful South Beach, it was going to be original, dangerous, and funny.

Mitch was a respected journalist who had written some excellent unproduced screenplays. O'Donoghue, thin, bald, usually sporting ballet shoes and a woman's diamond evening watch, was notorious, even with this look, for chasing young girls. He didn't start out with any aspirations of being a Hollywood screenwriter. He was the original head writer of *Saturday Night Live,* where his temper was legendary. He was intractable, merciless, self-destructive, but, above all, very talented. The writing team had a yin-yang, good cop–bad cop quality to it. Special handling would be required. O'Donoghue was clearly the loose cannon.

When *SNL* went into a menopausal lapse from the loss of Belushi, Ackroyd, Gilda, Chevy, and others, O'Donoghue and the producer, Lorne Michaels, both retired from the show. Years later Lorne returned and rehired O'Donoghue to revive *SNL.* O'D's first assignment was to write the monologue for Chevy Chase. As a returning *SNL* legend and host, Chevy was looking for something special to start off the evening. Since Chevy had left the show, he had acquired some success in movies, but the daring and original comedy that had made him a star on *SNL* had clearly waned. Although there was no love lost between Chase and O'Donoghue, O'D's monologue would assuredly revive Chevy's comic edge. Right before Chase was to go out for his first audience rehearsal, Michael presented the monologue to him and the anxiously waiting staff:

> Right after I stopped doing cocaine, I turned into a giant garden slug, and, for the life of me, I don't know why. Hi, I'm Chevy Chase. Have you noticed that, in the years since I left *Saturday Night Live,* my eyes have actually gotten smaller and closer together, so they now look like little pig eyes? Why? Again, I don't have a clue.

With unyielding shock comedy, O'Donoghue reviewed Chevy's film career and finished the monologue with:

My next film is called *The Giant Garden Slug Blows Eddie Murphy While John Candy Watches,* and it opens tomorrow at Red Carpet theaters everywhere. Don't miss it.

Chase, of course, was stunned, and Michael unflappably refused to do a rewrite. Somebody else wrote a new monologue.

A week later *The New York Times,* in a story covering the "new" and "revived" *SNL,* asked O'Donoghue what his reaction was to the show. He said blithely, "It was like watching old men die." His writing services were soon terminated.

Trying to harness some of this untamed comic energy, I set up a deal with O'Donoghue and Glazer for a first draft and two sets of revisions with Universal. Based on this history, one would assume that getting any revisions from this twosome would be a little shaky, but I was counting on Glazer's sanity to be my bargaining chip. For the record, this was a rather simple deal to put together. The young executives Sean Daniel and Bruce Berman knew the quality of Mitch's work from his past screenplays. Michael, of course, had writing cachet from *Saturday Night Live.* And I had already produced a few minor hits for the studio (e.g., *Car Wash, Fast Times at Ridgemont High, Melvin and Howard*). The studio had confidence in the "team." Naturally, this allowed the acceptance of a much shorter pitch.

Within four months Michael and Mitch had completed the first draft. It started off as a producer's dream. As I slowly read the pages, I howled, I broke into a sweat, I even started to count the box-office receipts. But two thirds into the script I hit a snag. It seemed like there must have been some mistake. I thought maybe I had misread the pages. I went back ten pages and continued to reread. No. I was right the first time. On page seventy, with fifty pages still to go, the gorgeous, lovably daffy Joy was viciously stabbed to death by a giant Trident. There was no mistake, she was not going to return. Her blood was spilled. No tricks here; the heartbeat had stopped. It was sort of like disemboweling Bambi as he was trying to find his mother.

I reread it for the third time, but sure enough she was still dead. Needless to say, this was a big crack in the Hollywood dam of do's and don'ts. Even the most forgiving reader, after being slowly lead down the primrose path, half-expecting at the very least to see an unrequited love develop between Crews and Joy, would be forced to abandon the script. For a film executive, this approach was suicide.

Naturally, I went to Mitch, the milder of the two, to attempt to get this incident changed before submitting the script to Universal. Straining to remain poised and professional, I explained, in great detail, the brutal concept of development hell.

"Mitch, what the fuck am I going to do with a script where the heroine dies in the middle of the movie?"

"It was a choice that we made after much discussion. After all, it is Mickey Crews's movie," he said.

"Read my lips. When the studio reads this, they will never get to the finish line."

"Let me talk to Michael and see how he feels."

"Feels!"

"The first draft took a lot out of him."

Mitch and I knew that to keep Joy alive for another fifty pages would be a lot of work. He would be no more eager to do it than Michael. Mitch called back two hours later and said that O'D would consider more work, but only after it had been read by the executives and he heard what they had to say. This was a man who gained a reputation for sticking knitting needles in his eyes on *SNL* doing an imitation of Richard Nixon in pain. I was not going to change his mind.

The writing duo flew to Los Angeles. We met on the eleventh floor of the black tower on the Universal lot. Knowing that O'D was a live wire act, Daniel and Berman carefully kept their eyes on him as they sadly began to discuss the problems in the script. There was a rather somber tone rarely seen at a meeting about a comedy. They couldn't rebound from the vicious killing of Joy. They politely queried things like "death?" "bloodshed?" "funny?" In the end, they had no alternative but to offer us a set of notes with the predictable message: "Try harder."

Mitch, O'Donoghue, and I drifted to the Universal commissary to discuss our next move over lunch. In retrospect, I realize that a studio commissary is not the best place to eat if your meeting does not go well. As we were seated in the public section, we watched Daniel and Berman being escorted to the power section in the rear. They must not have seen us, because when they glanced in our direction, there was no evidence of familiarity. When I'd initially discussed screenwriting with O'Donoghue, he claimed that Hollywood had been created by some old Jews for the sole purpose of torturing writers to get even for their own abysmal educations. The fact that movies were occasionally made was merely a sidelight. For him, this meeting was business as usual. Mitch was smart enough to see the future. Rewrites and spats with O'Donoghue and me were going to continue for months. Even he didn't realize it might take *years*.

We didn't discuss *Arrive Alive* or the meeting for over an hour. The jet lag had started to set in from their flight from New York, and it was clear that O'Donoghue's temperament had soured. But, after the sandwiches were eaten, I couldn't resist. I gazed over at Michael and said, "I told you so."

"It did get their attention, though, didn't it?" he said. The thought of executives in anguish made him smirk.

"But, Michael," I said. "You're writing for Hollywood. What difference does it make? When you slaughter Lassie in the middle of the movie, what can you expect?"

"If you wanted a *romantic* comedy, you should have said so! No one said *romantic* comedy. We told you it was going to be an *adventure* comedy."

"Maybe, but you poor bastards are now in hell. You are going to get numb from rewriting." I could not contain myself.

Mitch sighed. It was a sustained, billowy sigh, as the realization of spending months in the room with O'D began to set in.

"You tell me you know structure, well, I know Hollywood," I said. "This fucker is going to cost twenty million dollars to make, and you killed her on page seventy! For God's sake, let's at least get the ball into the strike zone."

"The strike zone!" O'Donoghue shrieked. That was it. He stood up and started pounding the side of his leg with his fist over and over again in some odd masochistic gesture that did not bode well for future revisions. Now I was certain that lunch had been a bad idea.

"The strike zone! The strike zone! Motherfucker, I invented the strike zone!" His face was scarlet, forcing Mitch and me to hold back that inexorable laugh that erupts when events are clearly at their darkest.

I could see Daniel and Berman finally eyeing us from the back of the commissary. They seemed quite relieved that they were sitting in the higher-priced section.

Lunch was over.

Well, *Arrive Alive* did, indeed, go into development hell, but its saga continued with a raging fury. Because there is such a shortage of truly inspired material, a good script can get sidetracked, but it is very hard to kill it off. After several unsatisfying rewrites, Universal put the screenplay into turnaround.

For those of you unfamiliar with this term, it simply means that the studio gives the producer a period of time (ninety days to a year, whatever is negotiated) to set the script up elsewhere and to return part or all of the costs that the studio has incurred. Sometimes there is a change of elements clause, which means that if one of the elements that they tried to attach to the script later agrees to do the movie, they will still have the opportunity to finance it. A change of elements was not part of my agreement.

Arrive Alive eventually made its way to Paramount Pictures, where it was given new life. The script was scarred but still kicking.

In the section where I discuss the packaging of movies, I will return to this saga. You will see how a good script can get made for the wrong reasons and then get mercifully shut down, in the middle of shooting, for the right reasons, leaving many dead bodies rotting in front of the Melrose gates.

DOSED AT THE JEROME BAR

The lesson: whenever your writer begins his out-of-town research and graciously asks you to join him, *don't*.

Landing in the Aspen airport during the end of March was very dreary. The skiers were gone, and the weather hadn't quite turned to spring. John Kaye and I were taking a short cab ride to the old Hotel Jerome, where we were to meet Dr. Hunter S. Thompson (our technical adviser) and begin the research for *Where the Buffalo Roam*. John and I went to Berkeley together and had collaborated on two movies. Neither *Rafferty and the Gold Dust Twins* nor *American Hot Wax* was considered a hit, but I thought John, who greatly appreciated the nightmare of Gonzo journalism, would write a good screenplay. Kaye was a little skeptical of the Doctor's wild reputation. He came to see if it was the product of pharmaceutical indigestion or merely hyperbole. I assured him, after my debacle with Thompson at the Beverly Wilshire Hotel, that he should stay alert and keep his eyes always on the road. I knew that if you have to visit Hunter on his home turf, it is wise to bring a friend.

"Are you the guys looking for the Doctor?" a tall, pretty local asked as she sat next to our table at the J Bar.

"Yeah, for about three hours," I said.

"Well, he's not in town. He's off in Chicago giving a college lecture. He won't be back till tomorrow, but he wanted you to have this."

She slid a small white packet of cocaine to John, wrote down what plane Thompson would be arriving on tomorrow, and told us if we needed anything that she would be next door.

"That's awfully nice of him. I guess this shows his southern hospitality," John said, demonstrating that he had already done some research and knew Hunter was from Kentucky.

"If you ask me, he waited a day just to soften you up," I said. I had seen the Taser gun.

As Thompson came off the plane, he was raving at some stranger, and clearly in a sour mood. He was carrying several suitcases and was dressed in his classic attire: large, colorful shirt; L. L. Bean walking shorts; Converse tennis shoes; and a cigarette holder clenched in his teeth. After brief introductions, we walked to my rented Buick, which was in the loading zone, sandwiched between a pickup truck and a shuttle van.

"No, no . . . I better drive, I know where I'm going," Hunter said, as I started to open the driver's door. Kaye got in the back. Hunter put the car in reverse and, in order to get more room to navigate, immediately slammed into the airport shuttle van behind him. The van bounced back three feet and settled. John shot me a startled look, but it was pale compared with the look from the driver of the van filled with tense tourists. Before an altercation was even possible, we had peeled out and were heading toward the closest liquor store to pick up supplies.

We were now heading to Woody Creek at an unbelievable speed. Clenched between Hunter's leg was a makeshift ice bucket with a bottle of Chivas; a brown bag filled with beer was on the seat.

"Do you still have any of that stuff from last night?" Thompson asked. Pussies that we were, he knew we wouldn't have finished it.

John, who was rendered almost speechless by the high-speed, squealing turns, handed Hunter the packet of coke and whispered, "You have got to slow down."

"You're safe, *goddamnit!* I'm prouder of my driving than I am of my writing!"

Everyone has gone seventy-five miles an hour, but not around hairpin turns in a Buick with shit suspension, driven by a casualty with a death wish. John's face looked like he was willing to settle for a minor accident, something like bashing into one of the tall eucalyptus trees or careening into a roadside hill, anything that would bring the car to a halt without inflicting severe bodily harm. Luck was on our side. We shot passed a sheriff's deputy at such a high speed that he was dumbfounded. As he blasted his siren, John, in midpanic, started eating the drugs while vainly shoving the open liquor bottles into the seat crevices. I was thinking that handling the inevitable narcotics charge would be a welcome relief.

When the cop approached the window, Thompson, with a Dunhill gripped in his teeth, turned to show off the famous Aspen profile, thinking that his face was a backstage pass to mayhem in Colorado. Unfortunately, this cop didn't recognize him and returned to his car to make a run on Hunter's license. Unworried, Hunter said, "He must be new around here." After all, six months earlier he'd almost run a successful campaign to become sheriff of Aspen on the promise that all his deputies would be encouraged to eat mescaline while on duty. His ascendancy would have allowed him to carry a holstered handgun in public to maintain law and order.

When the cop returned, he humbly apologized for unnecessarily detaining us. Thompson, after mumbling words to pardon the cop for his stupidity, screeched away toward Woody Creek.

Over the next thirty-six hours, John and I soaked up as much info and local color about Thompson and his life-style as anyone deserves to know. With no sleep, little food, and a barrage of chemicals, we finally wound up at the Jerome Bar at three in the morning. I was no longer able to stand or even sit up unless propped against an immovable object. John's eyes were bugging. He seemed to have lost his ability to blink. Thompson was playing a song, for the twentieth time, by the Amazing Rhythm Aces about a Civil War soldier who had his leg shot off. Was this some dreadful omen?

Mercifully, a cab dropped us at the airport at 5:30 A.M., three hours before our flight. The place was empty. John and I leaned against an outside wall near some bushes. We were both miserably jangled, and there was only one Valium left. We argued briefly about who needed the Valium more, knowing that if we split it, neither of us would be helped. I committed a selfish act that I have since felt bad about. While John was making his case, still bug-eyed, I grabbed the pill from his palm and downed it. He was too weak to fight.

Wise men would have learned from this experience and quickly abandoned any notion of making this into a movie. But I was a tenacious producer who was determined to go much further. I decided that not only should we make this thing but I should *direct it!* Excessive stimulants fueled my insatiable hubris to produce, to direct, to do everything.

We will return to this tale, because there is much more to learn here than merely the cardinal rule that A PRODUCER SHOULD NEVER HIRE HIMSELF AS A DIRECTOR BECAUSE THEN HE HAS NO ONE TO BLAME.

Part II

PRODUCTION

*It's not my fault . . . it's not my fault . . . it's not my fault
. . . it's not my fault . . . it's not my fault . . . it's not my
fault . . . it's not my fault . . . it's not my fault . . .*
—Rick Moranis imitating a movie producer
in the movie *Head Office*

THE PACKAGE, THE BUDGET,
THE STUDIO

WE ARE THE MAYONNAISE

You're about to graduate.

That script you have been developing is finally ready to be made.

Hopefully, that story you loved has not been so twisted during the development phase that you no longer recognize it. It wouldn't be the first time, for instance, that one started with a Western and the entire concept was changed along the way. After you are told that people on horseback don't sell tickets, or that the rich rancher if played by a woman would be more current, or that Wall Street has more power than a Winchester, your script inevitably gets a bit turned around. You get the drift.

Compromise is another word for playing ball. It's no longer about cowboys. You now find yourself trying to package a modern-day lesbian thriller, with romantic comic overtones. And, *even you* believe it's timely.

Maybe you shouldn't complain. After all, the script does exist, and, after reading the fourth set of revisions, even a couple of the executives have started to quiver and coo. This is a very delicate stage you are entering. Remember, at this point the studio is stuck for very little money, let's say $100,000 for all the writing services and $25,000 for your able supervision and gift for rapprochement. Even if you double or triple this number, it would be a mere pittance for the studios. They spend more money than this flying their friends around on weekends on their luxury G-4's.

Screenplays by comparison are relatively cheap.

If the studio backs out now, no real harm is done. It will be quickly forgotten by everyone but the writer.

What you are about to ask them for, I promise you, will get their attention. There is very little "give" between the script phase and the production phase. Once the studio obligates to a star or a director and starts building sets, it is too late to turn back. Suddenly, from nothing, tens of millions of dollars are at stake, and if that money is lost, it will be remembered. The top five grossing movies along with the dogs are listed regularly on "Entertainment Tonight." Figures proclaiming which studios are winning and losing are put in magazine racks next to the *National Enquirer*. Even housewives know that MGM is always having a bad year.

The executions are public.

To get to the heart of the beast, the producer must discern that there are two industries working side by side in Hollywood—making movies and developing movies. Unfortunately, the two seldom have anything to do with each other.

The development industry is where hundreds, even thousands, of scripts get developed without a prayer of being put on film. The closest these writers and producers get to a movie set is when they are driving to work and they accidentally spot the catering and equipment trucks parked on San Vicente.

This development process generates a massive amount of economy as well as unmentionable waste. Many deals are made. Agents dine. Lawyers are paid for their counsel. Executives, while they are in negotiations for their vacation homes, meet hourly to discuss scripts in development or about to be in development. Writers sometimes support entire families on script deals for years without ever seeing their names on the screen. Maxfields, the trendy clothes emporium, flourishes. All restaurants north of Beverly Boulevard are grateful. The cellular phone industry would wither without it. Even heart specialists in Beverly Hills cash in on this development industry.

But, sadly, movies rarely result from this process.

Thousands of people in L.A. meet daily for breakfast, to read the trades, hoping one of their friends was either fired or put in turnaround. They gleefully take relief that they were narrowly missed by the 10,000-pound Hollywood ax. Headlines like FOX CLEANS HOUSE, GLICKSBURG AND MYER ARE OUT, TWO PICS CANCELED can warm the belly. Chiding fate, the readers resume their dreadful litany of propping up bad ideas, wishing for that development deal so they can get in the game. After all, if a producer has enough scripts in development, he can earn sufficient income from development fees to survive without going into production. As I mentioned, a supervisory fee for bringing a development deal to a studio can range from $25,000 to $50,000 and more. Hey, if you have ten of these deals, you can "live." Twenty, and you can afford to give to charity. Why bother getting a movie made? Believe me, everyone is in on this.

Look at it from the movie executives' side. They can only make a mistake—a real mistake—when they champion a movie that gets made and fails. So long as a script stays in development, they can keep busy with rewrites, meetings, and phone calls, and the risks remain small. These men and women are not just fancy dressers. They are smart, overworked, dedicated, and often blamed for a bad decision that was really made by someone above them on the corporate ladder. There are scores of young executives whose careers bounce around like a bad amusement park ride. Some come and some go. Others seem to leap from studio to studio, scarred from the hot seat.

I have actually seen bodily and facial tics develop within eighteen months of an executive getting his job. Twitches of all kinds begin to soar. Eyelids begin to flutter. Upper lips dart sideways without warning. I remember one guy who quietly whistled while you were talking to him. I believe it was something from a Verdi opera. He was trying to listen to you, but he had this tune in his head that just had to come out. That's heat. That's pressure. To keep their jobs, these execs have to be very cautious.

Unfortunately, making a movie at any cost is not being cautious.

Whenever these guys have the guts to say yes, or the guts to implore their superiors to say yes, I salute them for going on the line, even if the movie turns out to be mindless fluff.

One of your most difficult tasks will be to get somebody to spend the money. Movies can be as cheap as a few million dollars, but if you want one that is "custom made," it can vault past $50 million. Because of overhead and union contracts, the costs for the major studios far exceed those for small independent companies, who can legally work with smaller crews at a faster pace. The *average* studio cost for each film, without including charges for prints and advertisements, exceeds $20 million. And this staggering number seems to double every ten years.

Executives are always looking over their shoulders, attempting to lowball budgets to protect their jobs. They serve not only a slew of senior officers but also a multinational board of directors. The result is that they are continually trying to control rumors of massive overages, because productions thought to be out of control throw a dim light on their ability to manage, compromising their ability to make future decisions. The process becomes very slippery with exaggerations. Speculations about actual money spent during production have run amok.

Lots of money is at stake, and with money comes power.

Let's be honest. Power is one of the major incentives that lures people into producing. If there is one image that most people associate with real power, it is that of a Hollywood Movie Producer. When you imagine a producer at the Beverly Hills Hotel, you envision a cigar-chomping, starlet-petting, pool-lounging power whore barking orders and getting people to look twice. Expensive cars. Fifty-foot swimming pools. Two housekeepers. It has become a cliché. *Power* and *producer* are words that seem synonymous. They are not.

Independent producers are no longer independent. We are sandwiched between those who have the money and those who control the talent.

We are the *mayonnaise*.

We may be barking orders while chomping on some stogie, but the only people who are still dancing to this power tune are cabana boys and topless waitresses. We are dependent, very dependent.

At present I am a producer who is exclusively contracted to Warner Bros. Pictures to develop and produce films for theatrical release. Independently, I can decide where I want to eat lunch and where I want to live. I can even, independently, select my own reading material for bedtime. When it comes to getting a movie made, however, *I have to ask.* Beseech. Cajole. Appeal. It's rather simple: the "asker" is never as powerful as the "askee." And we have to ask everyone for everything.

Studios for the money.
Agents for the talent.
Directors for permission to visit the set.
Ad pub guys for permission to look at the ad layouts.

Don (Beverly Hills Cop) Simpson, who always wanted to be the prima donna at the opera, the high-wire act at the circus, is rethinking his future. The money has not mollified his limp feelings. "Producing is the worst job in the world," he says. "When you're an actor, you get to play. When you're the writer, you get to stay home a lot. When you're the director, you're the *boss,* and everybody has to talk to *you.* When you're the fucking producer, everybody thinks you are a scum pimp who is not creative. It's terrible, and, in the end, you get blamed for everything."

I know this is starting to sound like producers are the Rodney Dangerfields of Hollywood, but the truth is we are a bastardized group without definition, without a clear mandate, without even a credit that anyone can understand.

Executive producer.
Producer.
Associate producer.
Co-producer.
A Joe Blow Production.

There have been some feeble attempts at explaining these, but they're all variations on a theme that spells *middle-*

man. There is such a thing as a "line" producer, who basically addresses the activity of budgeting, scheduling, and hiring the film crew. But for our purposes, this has nothing to do with the creation, development, packaging, and financing of a movie.

Confused identities and very little respect can lead to absurd frustrations. Stories about producers venting are plentiful. One producer shows his stuff by kicking down doors and throwing car phones through his window at high speed. Another waits until his assistant picks him up at the airport before telling him he is fired. As punishment, he takes his assistant's car, and the assistant is forced to make the long walk back to the city. Another runs around yelling at everyone except powerful studio heads. His favorite line is, "I hope you like pumps, because your next job will be selling shoes." Another is in a legal battle defending himself against the accusation of throwing metal objects at his female employees. Are these acts of power, or are they merely feeble attempts to get even for not controlling either the talent or the checkbook?

Indeed, if power ever was in the hands of producers, it has long ago slipped through our greasy palms. Things have gotten so bad that Peter Guber, one of our most renowned producers before taking over Sony Pictures (and hence getting real power), said while he was still producing, "A producer is just a dog with a script in his mouth."

In this climate, the only safe place for a producer to say "Fuck you!" is the privacy of his own home.

Is the concept of humility starting to come through here?

To be effective, you must understand how to use somebody else's money and still maintain confident appearances and some vestige of self-esteem. Your face becomes a death mask; a brash exterior (certainly the reason for the cigar, sunglasses, BMW, or Armani sport coat) to cover up the beady eyes and the grim, imploring mouth. Such maladies are shaped from not getting your calls returned and being told no on a daily basis.

Quite frankly, even Rodney has more power.

Very few producers are consistently well paid. Production fees range from $200,000 to $750,000 per picture, which seems like a lot of money, except for the fact that very few producers consistently get movies made. For most, it's less than one picture every three to four years. For the rest, it's more like one or two in a decade. And very few of these pictures become hits.

But all is not lost. Even though your power is a bit suspect, there is valuable work that can be done. To get the studio past development and into production, you have to find a way to help them justify the risk. No matter how snappy those script pages of yours seem to read, before big money changes hands, you and the studio are going to have to find some *elements*.

The last time I confronted the word *element* was in high school, when we had to memorize the periodic table in chemistry. It was a shorthand way to identify the elements in nature. In Hollywood, "Clint," "Marty," "Al," "Warren," "Steven," "Macaulay," "Barbra," "Penny," "Mel," and "Kevin" are all parts of our elements chart. Elements are those directors and actors who, when added to your script, reduce the risk factor for the execs.

It's no wonder that Mike Ovitz has become so powerful. He represents the people who give the studio the warm glow one gets from placing a bet on the right horse. It's a bum rap when people say Ovitz forces packages on these studios. They want them. They beg for them. "Barbra" makes hits. The fact that they complain that he charges too much is not his fault. They can always say no.

Without these high-priced "elements," studios are forced to make movies with less seasoned people, and if these movies fail, the finger will only be pointed more directly at the execs who green-lighted the productions. It is very comforting to be able to say, "Hey, his last three movies made a fortune, how was I to know he was over the hill already?" If you are an executive, would you rather have an $18 million movie starring Anthony LaPaglia and directed by Christopher Crowe or a $28 million movie with Al Pacino and Francis Coppola? You get it. If you insist on sharing the risks with the expensive talent, you have to be nice to Mike and say, "Please don't hurt me, I need you."

Trying to secure one of these "elements" while he or she is riding the crest of the wave can get very annoying. When I was packaging *Where the Buffalo Roam,* I tried to hire John Belushi to play the role of Oscar. Belushi was already sizzling from *Animal House* and *Saturday Night Live,* but flirting with Dr. Hunter S. Thompson was irresistible. I was granted a meeting with him at La Costa Country Club, where he was drying out. As I was getting in the car to make the long trek to San Diego, I stopped at a 7-Eleven for supplies just as the new issues of *Newsweek,* with John's face spread wide on the cover, were being placed in the rack. At once I knew that this was going to be an odd day for a meeting. No matter who you are, landing on the cover of *Newsweek* will make you dizzy, and Belushi was no exception.

By the time I arrived, there was already a long line of damp packagers waiting outside Belushi's door, each concealing his copy of *Newsweek,* and each grimly watching the others emerge from the star's bungalow, heads bowed after having received the sharp jolt of rejection. It was as if there was a neon sign above the door that said, "I am God, you are shit."

By the time I entered, Belushi's room was overflowing with savaged room service trays. Belushi was too tired and bored to make much of rebuffing me. He merely growled, "When you get a great director, maybe Scorsese, call me back."

His eyes said, "Next." I was too weak to say that I was the director.

Stars affect people, and it's no wonder that producers and studios seek them out. I have stood on my own movie set and heard passersby ask, "So, who's starring in this movie?" And I will say, for instance, "Paul LeMat." Their eyes get glassy as they turn to go down the road. While a movie is in production, it seems more exciting to have a recognizable name. Once the movie is completed, however, it only matters if it is good.

Fortunately, there are not enough of these big-time elements to go around. I don't know the exact figure, but well over one hundred movies are produced each year, and one hundred great directors and bankable actors simply do not exist. Creative choices that include untried people have to be attempted.

Herein lies the art of good producing.

You have to convince those with the money that these less than proven elements, who are willing to do your script, are really the first-rate elements of the future. The thing that saves you here, of course, is that the studios have to make enough movies to stay in business. They have vast distribution and theater divisions that must be fed. Eventually, they have to bite the bullet and go with the dimmer bulbs, with the hope that their wattage will get jolted along the way.

Recently, I produced *Point of No Return,* a remake of the French action thriller *La Femme Nikita.* Originally, Warners was hoping to get Julia Roberts to star; she was certainly an element that seemed to ensure box-office success. When she turned the role down, we decided on Bridget Fonda, who at the time was not a household name but was thought to be a "comer." Personally, I preferred her to Julia and was very happy with the result. But after *Pretty Woman,* if Julia had said yes, there would have been no chance in hell of selling Warners on the cheaper spread. Without much warning, their respective places on the elements chart may get reversed.

There are always arguments that you can use effectively to support your case. After all, when Bruce joined Tom and Melanie in *Bonfire of the Vanities,* millions of dollars were spent and the film never delivered the expected heat on the first Friday night. When you point to unforeseen successes like *Fried Green Tomatoes* or *Driving Miss Daisy* or *Home Alone,* be sure to mention the disappointment of *Hudson Hawk* or *Havana* or *Ishtar.*

Think how much money can be saved by coming up with less expensive but surprisingly effective choices. In fact, each year the results prove over and over again that expensive elements can backfire and hits can come from the most unexpected nooks and crannies.

Hold on to this argument very tightly.

Others can try to call Mike Ovitz or write the big check or buy the big names. But, for me, finding these unlikely packages and getting them made is the style and art of good producing.

Sometimes it works and sometimes it doesn't.

BLOW ME

Joy, the gorgeous, sweet, six-foot, curvy blonde who had retired from exotic dancing as the "Devil-Made-Me-Do-It Girl" to direct all her energies into selling real estate in Miami, was no longer mercilessly bludgeoned to death on page 70 of *Arrive Alive.* The writers, Mitch Glazer and Michael O'Donoghue, realizing the horrors of languishing in development hell, came to their senses and allowed her to live and join our seedy hero, Mickey Crews, for future escapades.

I have always had a special place in my heart for *Arrive Alive,* because it's a comedy that took some brave chances. It was dangerous by making you laugh when you weren't sure it was supposed to be funny, and it was bold by embracing characters who were on the ragged moral edge. Superbly written, it had its own peculiar style, which created many packaging problems. Finding the correct elements to justify the cost of production became a multiyear saga that eventually ended in doom.

Mickey, thirtyish, is a seedy detective working in a run-down, rat-infested Miami hotel, whose clientele is primarily old Jewish pensioners with an occasional brave tourist. Mickey and Joy meet at the hotel's 007 Bar, where Joy is grieving after the loss of her dog, Fluffy. We learn that Mickey is the one who kidnapped the dog, as an excuse to get close to the beautiful Joy. Here is a compressed version of their first encounter:

> *(Mickey glances down the bar at Joy, who continues to cry. Mickey grabs a lime off the counter. He takes a napkin, twists all four corners, and sets it over the lime. It's an old bar trick. He thumps the napkin with his middle finger, and we follow the thing as it wobbles all the way down the bar and bumps into Joy's arm. She stares at it tearfully as Mickey sidles up.)*

> MICKEY
> Hi, I couldn't help noticing—

                    JOY
Who are you?

                    MICKEY
Mickey Crews, head of hotel se-
curity. And of course this is my
friend, Mr. Bar Crab.

*(He smiles charmingly. She
bursts into tears.)*

                    MICKEY
Hey, c'mon. Here, take . . .

*(He reaches for his handker-
chief, thinks better of it, and
grabs a stack of cocktail nap-
kins.)*

                    MICKEY
. . . these.

(She blows her nose.)

                    MICKEY
Let's move over here where we
can talk.

*(They move to a booth beneath a
black-and-white poster of Ur-
sula Andress. As Joy gives
Mickey the description of
Fluffy, an old, leather-
faced woman wearing butter-
fly glasses sits at the next
table, smoking Satin ciga-
rettes and coughing her lungs
out. Mickey snaps at her.)*

                    MICKEY
        Would you mind dying at another
        booth?

OK. You get the gist. Mickey is a sleazeball, and Joy is gorgeous but naive. While Mickey is trying to put the make on Joy, he is also trying to find the the deed to some swampland that his murdered friend left behind. This juggling match leads to some dangerous encounters which eventually bring out the best in Mickey. The main difficulty with getting this up on the screen is that Mickey Crews requires an actor of the caliber of De Vito, who can be sleazy and lovable at the same time. His portrayal of Louie on "Taxi" was state of the art. De Vito didn't want to do it.

After failing to snag a couple of A-list directors, Universal lost interest in the material and put *Arrive Alive* into turnaround. I brought *Arrive Alive* to Paramount, where we continued to work on the development of the script and search for an actor and a director (more elements) that would satisfy management and me. At one time, Bill Murray, Michael Keaton, Dan Ackroyd, David Lee Roth, Kevin Kline, Morris Day (yes, Morris Day), Chevy Chase, Bob Uecker, and even Diane Keaton were discussed as candidates for Mickey Crews. Those creative meetings can get hectic and bent. Hugh Wilson *(Police Academy)* and Kevin Reynolds *(Robin Hood)* were directors who seriously flirted with the script.

When we had a director, we couldn't get a star, and when we had a substantial actor, we could never get a director. Over four years passed, and the packaging of *Arrive Alive* was becoming a weighty and impossible task. Ordinarily, the studio would get fed up and move on. But there were two very seductive qualities to this script that promised box office if it were well made. It had a lot of exciting action sequences, and it was very, very funny.

Meanwhile, I was off producing *The Untouchables,* *Scrooged* (which Glazer and O'Donoghue wrote after *Arrive Alive*), and *We're No Angels,* and I started to forget about Mickey Crews. The script was on the shelf. In fact, after years of turnaround by actors and directors, I was frankly hoping it would find its restful place in script development heaven. I was no longer pushing it.

"Guess what?" Gary Lucchesi, president in charge of production for Paramount, asked through the phone while I was finishing postproduction chores in London on *We're No Angels.*

"What?"

"Willem Dafoe wants to be Mickey Crews, and Jeremiah Chechik wants to direct. What do you think?" he asked.

"Well, Willem is an outstanding actor. He was brilliant in *Platoon* and a great villain in *To Live and Die in L.A.,* but can he make anyone laugh?"

"I don't know, but I think he's going to be a big star," Gary responded, hoping I would tell him not to worry, that we could make an elephant funny.

"Who's Chechik?"

"He just directed his first film, Chevy Chase's *Christmas Vacation,* and it's supposed to be a hit," he said.

"Has anyone seen it?"

"No."

Now this is a typical situation in playing the elements game in Hollywood. After years of getting frustrating rejections and still believing this script to be commercial material, we begin to flirt with a director whose work we have never seen but who might be a "comer," and with a prominent dramatic actor who has never been funny. One would assume that sirens would be going off: Wait! Rethink this! But, bear in mind, only a small percentage of movies can be made each year which on paper seem to have "safe" elements. There is only one Kevin Costner, and he can't make 112 films a year. Remember, taking chances with lesser elements is the only way a studio can ultimately fill up its slate of films.

Perhaps they were looking for me to say, "This is a car accident about to happen," but producers are simply not bred for this response. The struggle to get things going is so arduous and long that it softens the brain. Greed starts to massage your innards. Instead of becoming the devil's advocate, you find yourself able to justify anything.

I did what most would do, I mistakenly asked others who were familiar with the script what they thought.

"Art, don't forget, in Hollywood, three strikes and you're out," Brian De Palma cackled when I brought up the possibility of this package. That was all he could say; he couldn't stop laughing. I dismissed this reaction. After all, Brian is not known for making grand comedies. *I'm* funnier than he is.

"Do you think Willem could make you laugh?" I asked my wife.

"I saw him smile once and I had nightmares, but what do I know? Don't ask me," she replied. I only listen to my wife if she tells me what I want to hear. I'm trying to get a movie made.

The silliest thing you can do after these responses is ask the beleaguered writers their opinions. O'Donoghue took a long drag of some extra-thin, long, brown cigarette. "I like it," he said without moving his lips.

Glazer by this time was so burnt by the rewrites that ı could have sold him Gloria Swanson as Mickey Crews. He would have replied that whatever she lacked in comic timing she'd make up for in class.

I called the execs at Paramount with the cautious position that if Willem thought he could make this funny, maybe he could. A meeting was set up with Chechik, where I was supposed to discern whether he could make this movie, even

though I was unable to see the movie he'd directed for Warner
Bros.

A large man, he was dressed in a colorful mumu-type shirt
draped over black exercise tights, which certainly gave him a
comic bent. Other than a few TV commercials, I didn't have
much to go on. More important, he said that he knew Willem
from New York when Willem had been part of a theater group
that performed experimental comedies. He felt this could
work.

Christmas Vacation opened to substantial numbers. Although the work was rather modest, Chechik became the flavor of the month. Execs, Sid Ganis, Gary Lucchesi, and Bill
Horberg enthusiastically signed on, and Paramount committed
to the production. Because of the vast number of action sequences, the budget rested at a relatively high $23 million, even
before a really adequate location search could be made. This
usually meant that once we got to Florida and started building
sets, the number would begin to go up. It did.

As I drove up to the first location of what was to be the
interior and exterior of the De Soto Hotel, I got this strange
feeling that it was not as I was picturing it from the script. Even
though on the page it read:

> *The De Soto, one of the vast marble, mirror, and chande-*
> *lier behemoths thrown up in the boom fifties, has fallen*
> *hard. It is now simply big and sad.*

What I was seeing was so grim and real that there was nothing
humorous about it. When I walked into the lobby, an old, very
old lady banged her walker up against me while she was slowly
making her way to the elevator. "Move, damn it," she growled
as she cursed the movie business under her breath. Admittedly,
I hadn't come up with some brilliant alternative to this hotel,

but my gut was telling me that this was the kind of sad that makes you feel sad, that makes everyone feel sad. It's only funny if you live through it.

I asked Jeremiah if he felt as I did. He quickly and correctly pointed to the page that described the hotel as "the last and the sleaziest." As he gave me a commiserating nod, he folded his arms across yet another extremely oversized and colorful T-shirt which fell to his knees, just allowing the bottom of his pedal pusher tights to show. He was no longer wearing shoes.

"I guess we're in this together," he said.

It was summer in Miami, and I could feel the chill.

The next day Joan Cusack arrived, and my spirits were temporarily lifted. She is a truly gifted actress with great comic timing. During rehearsals, she was approaching the character with the light touch and whimsy of Judy Holliday.

The bad news was that the budget was rising rapidly. Action sequences that involved a killer whale combined with a large shoot out in the Everglades had been substantially underestimated. The production manager was now estimating $3 to $5 million in overages, and I thought he was low. I shared my concern with Ganis and Lucchesi, who felt it was too soon to panic. Once the horse leaves the barn, it's hard to get him back in.

Willem and Joan had never worked together before, so there was much anticipation on the first day of shooting. The chemistry between the two would be quickly evident. It was a charming little scene in Mickey's car. He has given Joy a necklace that he stole off some dead gangster, lied about why he had stood her up earlier, and is about to put her in mortal danger by crashing a big party to confront the treacherous villains. She thinks Mickey is big time.

*(Joy looks out at the line of
gleaming limos and the elegant
couples and sighs.)*

                    JOY
This is a pretty pulled-up affair, isn't it?

                    MICKEY
Believe me, it was a tough
ticket.

                    JOY
Maybe this was a mistake. Do I
look all right? I mean, how do I
look?

                    MICKEY
Like you could suck the date off
a dime.

Two days later, after seeing the dailies, I was more than concerned. It was not that the scene was badly shot or poorly acted but that it was creating a completely different set of feelings than what was intended. When Mickey said to Joy, "You could suck the date off a dime," it didn't make you smile, it made you cringe. You didn't want them to eventually end up together, you wanted Joy to jump out of the car and run for her life. Get out while she was still warm. No laughs here.

Three more sets of dailies came in, and my feelings hadn't changed. As I related this on the phone to Ganis and Lucchesi in Los Angeles, their voices became breathy and grim. I explained that if they were expecting to sell an action comedy for $30 million, they better be prepared to take the word "comedy" out of the ad campaign. Maybe it had been a miscalculation on our part, but scenes that we were laughing at on paper were deadly on the big screen.

I had gone along with (and was therefore responsible for) casting a combination that was not working. I was starting to believe that we had made a prodigious mistake. When I mentioned this, there was complete silence. If I was correct, there would be no expensive Navajo rug large enough to sweep this problem away.

Ganis cleared the lump from his throat and said, "Give it another couple of days."

"I can stay for as long as you want, but each day is very expensive," I said. "Maybe we should get another opinion, let somebody else look at these puppies. Maybe it's me. Maybe I'm just not in a funny mood."

They agreed to show the stuff to Tanen, who was no longer head of the studio but had stayed on as an adviser.

At night, I ate dinners with Mitch Glazer. I knew I was in deep shit when the writer, who was new at this game, started to question the tone of the movie. After the fourth day, he started to blurt out things like, "Well, maybe this doesn't have to be funny." Doesn't have to be funny! When I mentioned this to the executives in L.A., I could smell the sweat. Our career building blocks were starting to quiver.

It was a beautiful Miami morning; the oppressive heat was still two or three hours away. Mitch and I drove up to the hotel location to watch one of our favorite scenes come to life. In the story, Mickey has just escaped with his life after being captured by Indians living in the Everglades. Mickey had been spying on them, and he'd been beaten to a pulp. He has been up all night when he enters the hotel. Santella, the hotel manager and

Mickey's boss, has run out of patience. Mickey spends all his spare time baiting him.

> SANTELLA
> Well, that's it. He's out on his
> ass, I don't care. I'm sick of
> this. Even when he's here, he
> don't—
>
> *(Mickey stumbles in—pale,*
> *trembling, disheveled.)*
>
> SANTELLA
> Crews, I really hope somebody
> died in your family, because
> enough is enough, goddammit!
>
> *(Mickey walks right by him to*
> *the desk.)*
>
> MICKEY
> Got any Valium? . . . Codeine?
> . . . Tuinal? . . .
>
> DESK CLERK
> All I have is NyQuil.
>
> MICKEY
> I'll take it.
>
> *(The Desk Clerk hands him a bot-*
> *tle of NyQuil. Mickey unscrews*
> *the cap and carefully fills the*
> *little plastic cup with green*
> *liquid up to the measured dose*

*line. He sets the cap down on the
counter, then chugs the bottle.)*

SANTELLA

You get down there and take care
of the rats! RIGHT NOW! AHORA!
Or get the hell out of my hotel.

*(Mickey, after draining the
bottle, picks up the cup. Lift-
ing it high, he toasts Santella...)*

MICKEY

Blow me.

*(...and downs it. Then he heads
across the lobby.)*

As Mitch and I made our way past the crew and equipment, we watched while Jeremiah and Willem attempted different ways of saying "Blow me." Jeremiah said that maybe it
would be funnier if the emphasis was on *me*. "Blow *me*." Then
they tried emphasizing *Blow.* "*Blow* me." Then they tried whis-
pering it. Then they tried shouting it. No one was smiling. I
looked at Mitch; his eyes were watery. Everyone knows that
comedy is a serious business.

I booked a plane back to L.A. I wanted to discuss this in
person. I was going to put the unthinkable on the table. We
should rethink the casting, a sad option because Willem is truly
a talented man. Or face the fact that this very expensive movie
was going to be quite different from what we were expecting.
Or cut our losses now. I asked Lucchesi if Tanen had seen the
dailies. He said he wasn't sure who was in the screening room,

but after forty-five minutes there was a shout that sounded like Tanen.

"IRONWEED! IRONWEED! IRONWEED!"

Before leaving Florida I had discussed the strategy with Jeremiah. He was very understanding. To his credit, he also felt that the movie was taking on a somber and unexpected turn, but at this stage, the first week of shooting, a director is under siege. I don't know if it was conscious, but his shirts had become less colorful, almost drab. It was time for action. We decided that for the next three days he would shoot the killer whale sequence, just in case a casting change was imminent. The introductory scene involved an Indian princess who is accidentally eaten. It did not involve our principal actors.

I arrived in Los Angeles late Saturday for a 10:00 A.M. meeting on Sunday at the home of Frank Mancuso, who was then chairman of Paramount Communications. The meeting included Frank, Sid Ganis, Gary Lucchesi, and Bill Horberg, a young, bright, sad-faced executive who was already showing the signs of abuse that eighteen months in that job irrevocably inflicts. Some very tough decisions had to be made, but Mancuso, always a gentle and thoughtful man, kept the atmosphere positive.

Before the meeting started, we were all taken on a tour of his house, which had previously been owned by Khashoggi, the international arms dealer. The house was quite lavish and laced with marble. The effort to get past the awkward prebusiness small talk took on absurd proportions. We all ended up sandwiched in the small stone guest bathroom discussing the recent granite toilet acquired from Italy. It was evidently very old and rare. I looked over at Horberg, who somehow was being assigned much of the blame for this. He kept his gaze firmly on the bowl.

There was a very difficult business decision to be made here. The elements that we had assembled to make this picture, although each very talented in his or her own right, when combined with this script lacked the chemistry that Paramount was anticipating. It was supposed to have the light touch of *Romancing the Stone,* and it clearly did not. Stuff that made us laugh hilariously when read was dark and ominous on film. I felt then (and still do) that to justify such an expensive picture—and the costs were rising daily—the smartest thing to do was either to recast immediately and start again, or to shut down and absorb a loss that would be far less than that of finishing it.

Mancuso agreed.

Because we were unable to find a new cast quickly, the picture was stopped. It was a low point for me, but I felt that Paramount had made the brave and correct business decision. When I tried to reach Jeremiah to bring him up to speed, he was on the set at Miami's Seaquarium. It was already three in the afternoon, blazing hot, and he had yet to get the first shot in the can. Apparently, the killer whale was acting up. Jeremiah, still clad in a caftan and spandex peddle pushers, was now clearly overwhelmed and could not come to the phone. For the last five hours, he had been disconsolately perched in the bleachers overlooking the "whale bowl," limply clinging to his battery-driven megaphone. The stuntman, dressed in drag as the beautiful Indian princess, couldn't even get the whale to splash. Orca, not particularly concerned with the massive costs of an entire film crew forced to sit on its ass, was very cranky. He lay at the bottom of the pool, refusing to move.

We were told later that the whale would only cooperate if the stunt person was a beautiful woman.

Postscript: Jeremiah did not end up in the whale bowl for long. I ran into him in front of a magazine stand in Santa

Monica three years later. For a director, getting a picture canceled while it is still in production is usually the final, blood-
gurgling gasp. I wasn't sure if I was ever going to hear from this
guy again. As he rushed toward me screaming "Linson," my
first instinct was to deny my identity, but I was surprised to see
that he had not lost his bounce. He had added three more
earrings to his left lobe and wore an oversized T-shirt with
cartoon ducks on the front. Other than that, he seemed quite
the same. He told me that, after enormous pain and suffering,
he had finally been able to get another movie off the ground,
and he was in the process of editing it. I wished him well.

Six months later *Benny & Joon* was released. It became a
critical and box-office surprise. Wardrobe notwithstanding,
Jeremiah was magnificently unbowed.

THE GREEN LIGHT IS BLINKING

You can see that queer look in his eye. It begins just about four
weeks before the start of principal photography. One week
earlier there was a calm gaze, almost confident, a man in control of his destiny. He pranced through the commissary as if the
good grosses were tattooed to his forehead. One week later his
eyes grow furtive, his grin tightens, his self-assuredness is
faked. He is an executive who has just *green-lighted* a picture.
He has temporarily passed the baton of power.

Green lighting simply means that the studio has committed to the production of the film. The development stage has
concluded. There is no turning back. It means that the checkbook is open and all the enormous costs of filmmaking—
which include the hiring of crews, the building of sets, the
expenses for locations, the renting of sound stages, the manu-
facturing of wardrobe, the casting of actors—can begin. It

means that within a very short time literally millions of dollars can be spent and the likelihood that the studio will turn back is very, very remote. Once the production team smells this turn of events, the power subtly starts to shift.

A tribal dance takes place while the producer and the director await the green light. The studio, expecting to make this movie, wants to establish a budget that is as economical as possible. So long as major money has not yet been committed, the schedule becomes a negotiation. The less time it takes to shoot, the less money spent. No matter how many days the director and producer feel are necessary to complete the script, the studio will invariably require reductions.

Each day of shooting becomes a bargaining chip. On the one hand, the studio will attempt to pull pages out of the script or reduce the complexity of a sequence or require that a series of scenes get shot in a different location, all with the good intention of saving money. The producer and the director, on the other hand, are trying to preserve the integrity of the piece, trying to give the studio the best possible movie. It is sort of like that quiz show where one person says he can name that tune in five notes and the challenger claims to be able to name that tune in three.

"I can do it sixty-five days," the director offers.

"We are only prepared to make the movie if you can do it in fifty-five days," the studio counters, raising the possibility that unless the schedule gets shorter they won't be able to pull the trigger.

"How about sixty days?" The producer tries to compromise.

"Read my lips," the studio says. By now they are no longer looking at the producer; their eyes are fixed on the director.

"Instead of blowing up the bridge in three days, I'll get rid of all the dialogue and do it one," the director says, a little too desperately.

"How about replacing the bridge sequence entirely?"

"But."

"OK. You have one day," the studio counters, even though they have very little expectation that this task is possible. They feel they will save money by turning up the pressure.

Invariably, the filmmakers will cave, knowing they have agreed to a schedule, and hence a budget, that is virtually impossible to meet.

The producer may take a bolder stand, but doing so can be dangerous. Take this sequence of events. I was trying to get a green light for *The Untouchables*. After endless attempts, we couldn't get the budget down to the level that Paramount needed to make the movie. Finally, out of exasperation, I said to Dawn Steel, "Hey, it's gonna cost what it's gonna cost. If you don't want to make the movie, don't make it." She and Ned Tanen agreed to make it.

Two years later, when she was running Columbia and I was trying to get the green light on *Casualties of War,* we reached the same impasse. I said, "It's gonna cost what it's gonna cost. If you don't want to make the movie, don't make it." She agreed to make it.

Later, after leaving Columbia and becoming an independent producer for Disney, she was on the other side of the table when the schedule and budget for her movie hit an impasse. She decided to try my approach.

"Take more out of the schedule and budget or we won't make the movie," they said.

She gazed directly into their eyes and replied, "It's gonna cost what it's gonna cost. If you don't want to make the movie, don't make it."

"Fine." They canceled the picture.

And so it goes.

If costs balloon because everyone has simply agreed to an unrealistic schedule, then the blame can be shared by all. The execs are comfortable because they can tell their superiors that it's not their fault the production is going too slowly. Production can blame the false schedule. The ability to duck blame is a major asset in Hollywood. It is more important than the ability to read. Now everyone has a finger to point while nervously waiting to see if the sucker will work with an audience. If a movie is a hit, one rarely hears any complaints about being a week or two over schedule.

It is understandable why there's so much pressure at this stage. Once the picture begins photography, if the director takes longer to shoot than agreed upon, there is not a great deal the studio can do except hold on to their balls, pray for good weather, and hope that he or she picks up the pace. There is a famous John Ford story in which a young executive—I guess this was part of his hazing to get into the club—came on the set to warn Ford that he was one week behind. Ford took out his script and randomly tore out fifteen pages, handed them to the red-faced kid, and said, "Now we're back on schedule."

Replacing directors is very costly and very rare. But it has happened. Except for the most extraordinary circumstances (e.g., *Arrive Alive*) the only legitimate leverage the studio has after green-lighting the film is a veiled threat not to rehire the director or the producer in the future. Everyone has to be careful, because, in case the movie works, they want to maintain good relations. Therefore, the only viable option the studio has is to postpone the green light for as long as possible. The result is that you are often positioned to make a film with a schedule which both sides secretly acknowledge to be specious. Major heat and a lot of unresolved tension develop before and during shooting, as the days and the overages inevitably mount.

Relinquishing control can have a profound effect on studio executives who are trying to ride the elevator to the top floor. As a peculiar act of defiance, one young exec, after entering a meeting to announce to the director and producer that their movie had been green-lighted, actually unzipped his pants, put his soft member on the producer's desk, threw his hands up in the air, and said, "Fellas, the picture is a go." Was he saying "please be gentle" or "kiss my ass"?

I assumed he was offering his congratulations.

MUSICAL CHAIRS

This may sound strange coming from me, but most executives in Hollywood are hardworking, smart, and usually well intended. Occasionally, however, you can get trapped by reckless ambition. If you work in Hollywood long enough, you will come across a phenomenon known as executive musical chairs. Invariably if you are in the middle of this, you will get snakebit.

Here's how it works: you begin the development of a project with one set of executives, but by the time you've gone through the endless rewrites and meetings, you end up turning in a script to a whole new set of executives. The group that was "angeling" your script have long since moved on to other companies or gracefully retreated into forced retirement. The newly arrived executives have their own agendas. Your problems are compounded because when they come on the scene, anything left over from the prior regime is usually erased. They want to make their own imprint. They want to look good; this is rarely accomplished by making their predecessors look good.

In the final stages of my term at Paramount, circa 1989, I

was developing a comedy called *Fish Story,* a modern-day tale of a fallen but famous TV star, Terry, and his dolphin, Pepper, who continued to maintain a close friendship even after their show was canceled. They were so close that Terry could talk to Pepper. Their current misfortunes had turned them into a lounge act at a seedy bar in the Florida Keys, where they languished on the outer edges of show business. A series of adventures leads them back to the top. It was a terrific idea written by Mitch Glazer.

Mitch was just about to complete his third set of revisions in fifteen months, and the script was really starting to take shape. Ned Tanen and his staff were very excited about it. It was talked about seriously as a comedy for the following summer. Unfortunately, the executive winds were changing direction. The corporate politics at Paramount had hit a low. You could feel the chaos even in the commissary. The hostess was so confused by the influx of new management, she would continually screw up the daily table arrangement. Tanen, smelling the impending doom, had retired into an advisory role. This meant he was getting money to give advice but did not have to take any responsibility for the results. Frank Mancuso, who was running the place, was feeling a little concerned after having brought in Sid Ganis and Barry London to run the movie company. So he decided to beef up the film division by adding David Kirkpatrick.

Small and bald, Kirkpatrick was once a junior executive at Paramount, where he was mainly known for commandeering Joe Dante's *Explorers,* an expensive but unsuccessful hardware movie, before getting snatched up by Jerry Weintraub's Entertainment conglomerate to run the Motion Picture Division. Within twenty-four months, the company paid for and released *Fresh Horses, Troop Beverly Hills, Listen to Me, My Stepmother Is an Alien,* and *She's Out of Control.* Without a chance of snatching some life-saving oxygen from new investors, the hapless company staggered brutally into receivership. Kirkpatrick, seemingly drenched in Teflon, went on to a new job at Disney for even more money.

Things didn't go particularly well for him in the home that Mickey Mouse built, but the Disney management, headed by Jeff Katzenberg, was too strong and too smart to receive any mortal wounds from his presence. Astonishingly, Paramount sought Kirkpatrick back while he was still under contract at Disney. Because Disney was so undeniably successful under the control of Katzenberg, Paramount must have figured that what was good enough for Katzenberg was good enough for them. This was an error. It was also a classic example of the Hollywood executive shuffle performed as clumsily as a bad version of musical chairs.

There is such a dearth of talented film executives, companies are forced to resort to hiring—even trying to steal away—executives whose only legacy is familiarity with the players. These people move from job to job, often without much success. They are sustained by their ability to be moving targets with good fronts; rarely do they achieve much of a mark based on their personal contributions to movies. In fact, in most cases there's a trail of undiscussed disasters in their wake—those orphaned movies that no one seems to have had anything to do with.

During the first week of his reign, being very excited about *Fish Story,* I called Kirkpatrick to discuss the best way to get this film packaged. The last rewrite had just come in, and the initial reaction was excellent. I was quite aware of the importance of winning over a new regime with an old project. He apparently had just read the script as I entered his office. Without mincing words, he dismissed the script as sort of funny in a seventies kind of way but clearly "not hip and current." Since he was now the guy holding the checkbook, he quickly became the purveyor of *new*. He then spent an inordinate amount of time telling me how he'd started at Paramount in a little office at the end of the hall seven years ago and how everyone between that little office in the back and the grand one he presently occupied was about to see some changes. I assumed I was one of the ruts in that road.

I called him two weeks later to mention that Tim Robbins had just called and said he was interested in the material, that maybe we should meet to take advantage of his thoughts. Still drunk with his newfound mandate, Kirkpatrick said, "You're bothering me with this," and slammed down the phone. Within days I gratefully took asylum at Warner Bros.

My guess was that this contentious behavior would eventually do him in. Still, maybe this attitude was encouraged. It was a volatile time at at the company, where extraordinary events were operating on their own life force. Within a short time—six months to be exact—the entire Film Division would be ripped to shreds. When the dust finally settled, everyone—Mancuso, Ganis, Tanen, Lucchesi, Simpson, Jerry Bruckheimer, and even Kirkpatrick as an executive—was gone.

Does this section sound vindictive or instructional? Well, that question is always part of the cruel separations that occur when Hollywood power is being administered. Trying to get movies made, even if they are funny movies, can give birth to some nasty disagreements.

Meanwhile, *Fish Story* is still at Paramount, resting quietly on someone's shelf. Forsaken, but joined by countless other scripts, waiting for the newest administration to say, "For God's sake, don't we have any comedies in development for next summer?"

IF HE PULLS OUT A KNIFE, YOU PULL OUT A GUN

When you come face to face with Brian De Palma for the first time, it doesn't come as some big surprise that he directed *Carrie* and *Dressed to Kill.* He is large, abrupt, and seemingly stern. You are instantly given the feeling that if he hasn't yet scared the shit out of you, he eventually will.

I was waiting in my office for Brian to arrive so we could have our initial meeting with Paramount to discuss his interest in directing *The Untouchables.* I'd been warned by everyone that with the two of us in the same cage, I would last for about a week. My bones would be picked clean. Rumors abounded. On his last movie, *Wise Guys,* Brian had thrown the producer, Aaron Russo, off the set and off the picture. Supposedly, Aaron, who was standing on the sidelines while Brian was setting up for a shot, had walked over and asked Brian to go in for an additional close-up of Joe Piscopo. Brian slowly turned, and the steel curtain dropped. Within twelve months Aaron's name had appeared in the weekly *Variety*'s Missing Person Report. He had moved to the South Pacific.

I learned later that Aaron also had a nasty habit of grabbing your balls when you least expected it. It was an odd form of male bonding that in retrospect was a poor choice with Brian De Palma. Even though De Palma was known for having "balls," he didn't want them handled by producers.

I was optimistic.

One of the most exhilarating things about De Palma's movies is that they have an oversized, operatic style. If you recall the chain saw scene from *Scarface,* as the whirring blade gets close to the neck, you start to believe that you are seeing more horror than was even shot. When Brian kills somebody, you never forget it. When Brian decides to spare somebody, you don't forget that either. My gut sensed that if we could get him to impose this "aria" on a simple but well-written tale of good versus evil, he could bring a lot of unexpected weight and depth to a drama that was already well known. Just like Mamet, De Palma could push the envelope of an old television series to new and wonderful heights.

When Brian arrived, he was wearing one of those large safari bush jackets and, for those of you who haven't seen him on "Larry King Live," he was sporting a full gray beard. It was more than a Hemingway affectation; it suited him. Our first meeting with the folks at Paramount was gentle enough. We were still courting. All of us expressed our excitement about the project, acknowledging that more work on the screenplay was still necessary. (Whenever there's a loss for words, pick on the script.) Casting choices were thrown around, but not in any serious way. None of the actors who ended up in the movie was even mentioned. I do remember someone in the meeting suggesting that John Candy might make a good Al Capone because he was so large, but Brian made no objection. My mouth started to open, but he just looked at me and smiled. I smiled. He'd been through all this before.

The thing that is relevant for our purposes is that Brian wisely offered very little information outside his zeal to get started. If he had an agenda, he felt it was too soon to reveal it. His "take" on the script, which all these meetings hoped to reveal, was best left for the dailies. Years of experience had told him that the more executives have to chew on before the movie gets green-lighted, the more muddled the process can become.

That was fine for them, but I was quite concerned that *I* would be kept from the process, unable to contribute to the end result. As we walked to the parking lot, there was virtually no small talk until we got to his car. He turned and said, "We have a lot of work to do. This script needs to be addressed . . . and this picture is going to cost more than they think it is.

Let's meet tomorrow." This was an encouraging sign. He perceived me as being on the side of the picture.

I was.

Within a week, we had become very close friends.

As soon as the director's deal is closed, several things happen at once. In addition to working on additional rewrites and starting initial discussions about principal cast, the studio immediately tries to come up with a schedule and a budget on which all parties can agree. At this stage, it is truly a "guesstimate." It seems complicated, but it isn't. The process is divided into two parts:

- The *above-the-line* costs, which include the entire cast, the director's and the producer's salaries, and the final cost of all writing services.
- The *below-the-line* costs: for our purposes, everything else. This category encompasses all costs from the paper clips the producer chews on to the construction of million-dollar sets, from the hot lunches for the Teamsters to the rental charges for anamorphic lenses.

The reason I called it a guesstimate is that the below-the-line charges can expand and contract like an accordion, depending on a variety of decisions that cannot be made without a lot of investigation and planning. The director has to decide on where the movie is going to be shot (this requires several days to scout locations), the style in which he is going to shoot it (this includes the size and complexity of his action sequences, the amount of extras he needs to fill the streets, the number of sets to be constructed, designed, and dressed), and the cost of the cinematography, which can vary enormously depending on what cinematographer he chooses. To decide all these variables takes time, but before the studio spends any "real" money (e.g., getting on the road to green-lighting the picture) they want to get a "number."

There is no reason to get overloaded with unnecessary facts and figures, but it helps to set the stage for the strategy that Brian and I were faced with to get *The Untouchables* launched. Over the next few weeks, Paramount's budget department, working with our production manager, Ray Hardwick, arrived at a tentative number of $18 million over a fifty-five- to sixty-day shooting schedule. This number provided for a very tight above-the-line cast cost. Eliot Ness was $900,000, Al Capone was $200,000 (remember, at this stage Capone's role was half the size of that in the final draft), and Malone (Ness's mentor) was $500,000.

The schedule initially assumed we would do much of the movie in L.A. and include exteriors in Chicago to save money. Eventually it turned out that the cost of shooting it all in Chicago would be only slightly more, and the authenticity would be vastly improved. Brian never said that this schedule seemed light, but the look in his eye told me that he had a bigger appetite than a fifty-five-day schedule was going to allow.

I met Kevin Costner at Du Par's in the Farmers Market about a month before Mamet had finished the first draft. He was wearing a bomber jacket and air force shades. Steve McQueen was written all over his forehead. At this time he had gained a minor reputation for his supporting role in *Silverado,* but in the industry he was primarily known as the dead body in the opening scene of *The Big Chill.* Apparently, the picture was running too long, and Larry Kasdan had to lose the rest of his performance. Oddly, even though he'd ended up on the cutting room floor, his reputation was starting to take off. I told Kevin that I was developing the movie version of *The Untouchables* with David Mamet and that he would be perfect for Eliot Ness. He said he wasn't particularly interested in Ness, but he had read *Arrive Alive,* thought it was hilarious, and was interested in Mickey Crews. I threw back my coffee and said it was great to meet him.

Brian and I started working out of my office at Paramount, where half the day was spent on casting (meeting and reading with actors) and the other half on a budget that would attempt to live up to the "number" that Paramount was expecting.

We sent Costner the finished script with De Palma attached as the director. This time the unexpected writing with a unique director piqued his interest. Brian was coming off two movies (*Wise Guys* and *Body Double*) that were flops at the box office. Under the general rule that he later passed on to me, "three strikes and you're out," Brian wanted a hit. With the economics in Hollywood reaching such frightening levels, and the demand for higher and higher film grosses to please multinational corporations, a medium success is out of the question. It's nice, but it really doesn't get anybody excited. And real art gets so suppressed that within a short time staying alive becomes your primary consideration. The idea of Costner appealed to De Palma, but he was worried that Costner didn't have enough star power to ensure a hit.

We met with Mel Gibson, who eventually said no, and De Palma flirted with and then passed on the idea of Don Johnson. In the end, Kevin was such a good choice that Brian bit the bullet, hoping to shore up the marquee with the other supporting roles.

"We've got to get a movie star like Sean Connery to play Malone," Brian said to me before our first burst of actors' readings were to start.

"Why a movie star?" I asked.

"Because if I kill off Sean Connery in a movie, no one will believe it," he said as he came alive. Just the thought of Sean, blood spattered, slowly crawling down the hallway, desperate to make his final call, was giving Brian that big, broad smile that others get when they review their baby pictures.

It was a brilliant idea, but we didn't have enough in the budget to pay Connery's price. Connery was sort of in the same condition as Brian. He had been in some very successful films, particularly the James Bond series, and he had done some wonderful work, but his last several efforts had not been successful at the box office. Putting his name up in lights would not ensure restful sleep on that first Friday night when the movie opened.

Ned Tanen was clear. "If you want Sean Connery, he's going to have to do it for what we have in the budget."

Fortunately, this did not stop Sean from reading the script and getting excited about the part. Actors, more than anyone, appreciate the words. They're the ones who are left dangling in front of a camera when there is nothing worthwhile to say. Sean read Mamet, met with De Palma, and was hooked. For a short time negotiations were tense. Mike Ovitz said if we couldn't match Sean's price, which at the time was $2 million, he would rather do it for nothing and take a percentage of the gross at an early dollar position. Tanen agreed. With hindsight, it would have been cheaper to pay him his price.

So far so good.

If it is starting to sound like the producer at this stage is becoming a bit of a bystander, well, it's true. The studio has the checkbook, and the director thinks he has been mandated to carry out his personal vision. No one will say this to your face, but everyone at this point hopes you'll go off and start to plan the wrap party and design the T-shirts, jackets, and hats for the crew. This is why so many producers are thought of as screamers and yellers; you've got to make noise to be heard, because no one important is listening.

There is still a meaningful job to be done, but it is one of liaison and support. You can exert much influence by merely cautioning either side that the path being taken is the wrong one, or encouraging either side that the decision being made is correct. For example, Brian and I had set up production offices in Chicago and begun concentrating our efforts on the physical production of the movie: how long and how much. The wished-for number of $18 million was becoming a dim memory. As Brian was trying to find locations for the larger sequences, such as the stairs at the train station, or the shoot-out outside the courthouse, or the horseback drug bust in Montana, or the opera backdrop just to give Capone a message, it became clear that the picture he was gearing up was more ambitious than the studio was expecting. The budget started to escalate. It was eight weeks before shooting, we had just passed $19 million, and the picture was still not officially "green-lighted."

Tanen and Steel were getting concerned. They knew this was going to be the start of a trend. As the producer, I was quite excited about Brian's plan. Each step to me seemed to add so much visual power to the movie that I felt it was well worth the money. Of course, it wasn't my money.

There are two things a producer can do at this point: he can lie and say not to worry, the budget won't go any higher, or he can try to convince them that the movie they really want, the one that's going to make them look like geniuses, the one that they'll choose to list in *Variety* when they announce their next job, is simply going to cost more money, but money well spent.

I did both.

This approach bought us a moratorium for a few weeks, after which the budget would again get recomputed and the discussions would again reheat.

*   *   *

Andy Garcia is a very clever fellow. Brian and I wanted him to play Nitti, Capone's flashy assassin. We had seen him in Hal Ashby's *8 Million Ways to Die,* where he was one of the most electrifying new villains to appear on the scene. Even though no one had really heard of this guy, he refused to come in to meet. I was impressed. He said he didn't want the part of Nitti because he felt he had done it already; he wanted the role of Stone.

Stone was Ness's junior detective, who had very few lines in the movie. Actors have been known to count the lines. On the face of it, Nitti was the flashier and bigger role, but Andy was smart. There were many scenes where Stone's name was not even mentioned in the descriptive setup, but Andy knew that he was Ness's sidekick. Even if he wasn't saying anything, he would be standing there next to Costner and Connery. Brian would have to make sure he would do something, and from this he could build a memorable part. Just by wearing different colors and pacing back and forth, he would be noticed.

We told him he could come in and discuss the other part so long as he kept an open mind about Nitti. He came to meet, but he was firm. As annoying as this was, Andy was impressive, and we conceded on Nitti.

The clock was ticking, six weeks to go before we hoped to start photography. Ray Hardwick, who was responsible for organizing each detail of the budget and the schedule, appeared as if he would contract a serious case of eczema unless we did something about getting this schedule in line with the studio's expectations. Every seam was splitting apart. The number was starting to approach the scary plateau of $20 million.

The lighting package for the cinematographer, Steve Burum, had doubled.

The shooting days had increased by another week.

The costs of locations, set construction, and period set dressing had doubled.

The number of extras had increased and, because of the "period," wardrobe had increased.

"Brian, can you really do this sequence in three days?" Ray would ask while scratching his hand.

"If the gods are with us," Brian would say, perched in his chair, Buddha-like, almost enjoying the hysteria.

Tanen was not happy. And if Tanen, Steel's boss, wasn't happy, then Steel wasn't happy.

The only good news was that the above-the-line costs had remained the same. We had yet to cast Capone, but the rest of the cast was coming in on budget. We met with Bob Hoskins. He was interested in the role, and we could get him for the $200,000 that was set aside.

As I was being called back to L.A. to discuss these over-ages with the studio, Brian casually mentioned that he had heard from Robert De Niro, who'd expressed interest in playing Capone. De Palma had made his first full-length feature in 1963; *The Wedding Party* had starred De Niro, and they continued their relationship with *Greetings* and *Hi, Mom!* But that was a long time ago, and they hadn't worked together since. I had never met De Niro.

"Wow!" was all that I could muster.

"He'd be great," Brian said.

"I think that with the budget spiraling, this could really send them into a tailspin," I said. Brian threw out that wicked smile. De Niro's price was in the millions, and he was not known for putting on garage sales.

"HEAR ME, LINSON! I want you to listen very, very carefully," Tanen said. "We are not spending $20 million to remake a gangster movie. This picture is not green-lighted. This budget is soaring. Get it under control. Get the number down. And tell your director that he better start looking at himself in the mirror and coming up with the right answers." Tanen was spitting his words as his rant started to cool.

I knew, deep down, that Tanen really loved this project, but he had promised Mancuso and the board that it would be made for $18 million. As we inexorably marched to twenty, his expression was turning sour. If De Niro were added, we would be pushing $23 million.

When I'm standing on this platform, I usually like to say, "If you give us the extra two million, I promise you, cross my heart, all of this additional money will end up on the screen." This tip frequently makes everyone calmer, even though no one is sure what it really means. But Tanen is way too smart for this kind of bandage. Had I said it, he might have completely blown.

I could have tried the ever-faithful approach, "This is what it's going to cost. If you don't want to make it, don't make it." But there is an unconfirmed rumor that Tanen, in the heat of a bad budget meeting, once tossed a pencil in the direction of a producer and the pencil actually stuck in the guy's chest.

"Are you aware that De Niro is willing to play Capone?" I said, as I moved quickly to my left.

"Linson, you have $200,000 to spend. If I were you, I'd sign Hoskins before you lose him."

I was sent back to Chicago with a mandate. Cut your appetite. Cut your schedule. Fortunately for us, the clock was ticking, we were spending more and more money in essential preparation, we were slowly getting past the point of no return.

Usually at this point in the story, one hears how the producer gets on his hands and knees and starts to beg or scream or even weep. After all, De Niro is one of the greatest screen actors of all time. Rarely does a producer get a chance to have a front-row seat to watch (and ultimately take credit for) the work of someone so special. Bob De Niro as Al Capone. Get outta here! I had the feeling that if I were Joel Silver, I would have held Tanen at gunpoint until he submitted.

But it wasn't the right time. Tanen was in no position to be moved. And, strategically, from our point of view, there was still a small chance that the picture would be postponed or canceled. "Keep getting them pregnant" was the rule that De Palma and I were living by. The more money committed, the more the power shifts to the filmmaker.

There was still six weeks to go until we started shooting, and the Capone sequences were going to be shot at the end of the schedule. No matter what happened, it would be four months before any film would be burned on Capone.

One can understand Tanen's hysteria over the rising costs:

Occasionally the problem lies with the director. As a director gains experience, he starts to realize the endless possibilities for shooting any scene. The amount of coverage, the number of angles necessary to convey the scene can be limitless, checked only by one's imagination. The more clout a director has—and a director who has clout is a director who doesn't care whether the studio rehires him or not—may quite easily avail himself of many options which he may or may not need. He grows out of control and becomes wasteful. Without a well-conceived plan, he will overshoot the movie and try to work it out in the cutting room. This can literally inflate a budget as much as $5 to $10 million—the nightmare we all try to avoid. Usually when a movie is way over schedule, assuming it was correctly scheduled, this is the reason.

None of the above, however, applied to *The Untouchables*. Brian De Palma is one of the most prepared directors in Hollywood. He has come up with a computer program wherein he storyboards each sequence in brilliant detail. A storyboard is a visual blueprint of the script in which the scenes get reduced to cartoon frames. Brian can actually walk you through the film scene by scene on his computer. It becomes a sort of animated, stick-figured playback of the final movie. When the film is in the can, he gives his storyboards to his editors to guide them through the first cut.

De Palma doesn't like the filming part of the process. To him it is often a joyless grind, and, since he is so prepared, there are rarely any surprises for him. He is carefully executing a very detailed plan. Much of the creativity and artistry is completely thought out weeks before he arrives on the set. The good news for studios is that he wants to get it over with as soon as they do.

This budget was going over because the spectacular events that Brian had conceived were expanded versions of what was indicated in Mamet's script. The studio, not knowing precisely what Brian had in mind, was really in the dark. To make his version of the script would simply take longer than had initially been estimated. In the end, it would be these extravagant scenes which would be remembered and which, along with Mamet's dialogue, would distinguish the film.

Brian and I had found our favorite coffee place, filled with attractive college girls, about two blocks from the production offices and around the corner from the hotel. We would meet daily and commiserate over the expanding budget and the strategy to get Paramount to do what was, in the end, in everybody's best interest. The fact that Brian was feeling the pressure of the schedule made him enjoy even more my retelling of the squirming going on in Hollywood. He wanted to hear every detail.

When we held the line with Connery by telling him that there was no room in the budget to pay his full fee, he made a deferred deal. This meant that he would be paid later, depending on how the movie performed in the marketplace. Since De Niro was not at this time prepared to reduce his price, it would be sticky to pay his full fee, even if Paramount was ready. Doing so could easily reopen the Connery deal. We therefore decided to go with Hoskins. For us, he was not as electrifying a choice, but he was the only choice, and it was getting Tanen more pregnant. In fact, one could say he was entering his ninth month.

Two more weeks had passed. There were four weeks to go. Sets were being built, and the rest of the cast was pretty much determined. Brian and I were in the production office listening to a shoddy group of potential opera singers desperately delivering the aria from *Pagliacci* when I got the call from Hollywood. I was waiting for this.

The call came from an assistant. The budget had soared past $20 million and was edging to $21. Tanen was getting on the plane in the morning to go through the entire film, hoping to make cuts and stop the bleeding. He suggested that this would give us twenty-four hours to come up with a plan. He was obviously pissed off.

I returned to the production office to find De Palma slumped in his chair with a chubby actor down on one knee, inches from Brian's shoes, lip-syncing *Pagliacci* from a bad cassette player. I looked at Brian, and he knew that the fun and games were over. To make matters worse, we had just heard that De Niro would consider deferring a million dollars of his salary. He really wanted to be Capone.

The thought of having to rescale the picture and do it without De Niro left us both in a deep funk. Instead of reveling in the usual gallows humor, Brian retired to his room. We did not speak, nor did Brian return to the office, until Tanen and his two assistants arrived the following afternoon.

What I did next should have occurred to me weeks before. When Tanen and his group arrived, and before the fireworks were to begin, I escorted Tanen around the production facility, where one could see the various elements from the script starting to come alive. The wardrobe department was filled with clothes from the thirties, the prop department was strewn with guns, badges, watches, and so on. We drove to several location sites to see how Chicago in the thirties would be recreated. The final stop was the large office that Brian and I occupied. On one wall were photographs of the cast. On the wider wall were photographs and detailed drawings of each set, laid out scene by scene. Here the extravagance of Brian's approach could be more easily visualized and understood. The executives could discover for themselves that this was becoming more than just a number on a top sheet, that months of preparation and thought had gone into the design of the picture. To their credit, they were affected by the depth of the work. Everything hanging on the walls looked exciting and real. Tanen, in particular, was warming up.

It was unmistakable that Brian had agonized over every sequence, and he was in no state of mind to pull back. With the poor outcome of his last two pictures still lingering, he was in no mood for compromise. He was standing at the plate with two strikes. He wanted to take a full swing. He was not going to bunt for a base hit. This was going to be his final battle. If this movie was going to get fucked up, it was not going to be because he scaled things down. He was determined to go to the hilt or get shot down in flames.

I was completely supportive. For me it was a chance to make a great picture. As a producer, you rarely get that feeling. It's so tough just to get one of these movies going that by the time you're ready to start, so many sacrifices have been taken that greatness is not usually a consideration. You just hope to get out with your tail intact, able to fight again. But this time it felt different. If our excesses could be granted, this movie could go beyond what the studio was expecting. Not only would we satisfy their need for box-office grosses but also it was a chance to give them quality, prestige, and a film to be proud of.

Six people—Tanen, his two assistants, Ray Hardwick, Brian, and I—took seats in the middle of the office surrounded by the *Untouchables* artifacts. There was some initial small talk. I could see that Tanen was slightly softened, taken by the richness of the photographs and architectural designs that we were about to implement.

For those of you who dream of becoming great strategists at meetings, keep an eye on Brian. His behavior may have been just a spur-of-the-moment and uncalculated action, but Brian, who had yet to enter into any conversations, started the meeting by asking people to leave the room.

"Ray [the production manager, the man who had all the facts and figures], could you excuse us for a moment?" he said.

Ray got up and left.

He then turned to Tanen's assistants and, incredibly, said, "I'd like you both to step out as well."

Tanen was surprised but didn't object. The young execs looked at me, afraid to object to De Palma, and slowly walked out of the room. Since the guy with the budget was no longer in the room, Tanen knew that this was not going to be a meeting about shortening a schedule. It was time to pull out all the stops.

"We have the opportunity to get De Niro to play Capone. I believe if we stay with the cast we have, shorten the schedule, and reduce the scale of the picture, that you will end up with a movie that at best will be suited for 'Masterpiece Theatre.' It is not the movie I want to direct. It will not work, and I cannot afford to make a movie that will not work." Brian said all of this quietly. He was clearly serious. *The Untouchables* was his last chance, a Custer's stand. He needed to shoot his entire arsenal on this one. He wanted no room for failure.

The room was still for about thirty seconds.

"Ned, think of it, when Bob De Niro kills somebody with a baseball bat, with Brian directing, it will never be forgotten,"

I added, trying to toss in something to break the ice. Ned kept his gaze on Brian.

Finally and thoughtfully, Tanen said that he heard what we were saying and would go back and talk to "his people," which meant he wanted to think about it.

Within a week, De Niro was hired, Hoskins was paid off in full for his pay-or-play commitment, and we were given an official go. What had started as an $18 million movie ended up at $22.5, but its chances for greatness were logarithmically enhanced.

THE CAST

WHAT IF HE GETS HIT BY A BUS?

After the hell the studio has put everyone through, by the time you get to the casting of a movie, you would think that the fun was about to begin. The producer gets to sit around listening to actors read from the script and decide who's going to be in the movie. Entertaining stuff? Perhaps.

With television and movies in our faces around the clock, everyone is accustomed to watching and evaluating performances. No matter who you are, it's natural to feel a certain amount of expertise when it comes to acting. "He's funny," "she's great," "they stink" are decisions that children as well as adults make every day as they attempt to analyze their daily dose of entertainment. Everyone believes he can do this job, if only given the chance. Casting, like almost every other phase of filmmaking, depends on instincts and taste. Making mistakes and watching others make mistakes is the only experience one gets. But what you think you see at a reading is rarely what you see on the screen. Choosing the right actor for the right part is harder than it looks, and reading an actor may or may not be a complete waste of time.

One of the difficulties in casting *This Boy's Life* was that the largest part was to be played by a teenage boy, who during the course of the film must age from fourteen to seventeen. Even though we had already cast Robert De Niro to play his stepfather and Ellen Barkin to play his mother, the ultimate success or failure of this film would rest primarily on the teen actor's abilities. Because of his age, there were no "stars" from which to choose, so the challenge of finding somebody new was at hand.

After the director, Michael Caton-Jones, a Scotsman (who on very rare occasions breaks tradition and buys everyone a round of drinks), and I narrowed the field to ten actors, De Niro flew to Los Angeles to read with them. We videotaped these sessions. When the last actor finished, Bob reached for a phone, made two quick calls, moved to the door, and said, referring to Leonardo Di Caprio, "I like the kid that was second to last." Michael and I had liked him too, but there were several others who'd also stood out as we were watching Bob engage them.

Later, when Michael and I had a chance to examine the tape, we saw that Leonardo's performance was more riveting, more subtle, and more emotional by far than the rest. The tape revealed to us a sensitivity that watching the reading live never did. Bob's decision was made without hesitation; his instincts were impeccable. Leonardo's performance speaks for itself.

Joe Pesci claims he has never gotten a job by reading for a part, whether live or on tape. Early on Joe would avoid auditioning unless he was desperate. Now that he has some clout, he flatly refuses to read, regardless of the role or the director. Joe says that it takes him months to prepare for a role, painstakingly working out each detail. He simply comes off wrong when asked to come in cold and look over some pages. Almost every actor will give you the same speech.

This is fine for Joe, but how are producers and directors supposed to tell if someone is right for the part if he or she won't read and there is little or no film on the actor? When I asked Joe he said, "Sit and talk with the actor about life, about the weather, about sex, about anything. When he talks to you, if he is full of shit as a person, then he will be full of shit when he acts . . . and by the way, the fuckin' reverse is true too." This might not sound like much, but there is probably some truth in it.

When Sean Penn came in to read for the role of Jeff Spicoli, the surfer in *Fast Times at Ridgemont High,* he stammered, flopped around like a beached carp, was barely audible, turned red, and said, "I really don't like to read." We didn't have anything else to go on. The only movie he had done was *Taps,* and it wasn't going to be released for months. We urged him to try again. He got more awkward and withdrawn and tried in vain to finish the scene. It was too painful to watch. I looked at the floor. His gnarled face turned toward the door. Other than his eyes, he was virtually limp. Amy Heckerling (the director) and I politely thanked him for coming in, and he left. Defying any logic, all of us in the room quickly agreed he should have the part. *There was something about him!* We jumped in blind, and to this day I can't seem to articulate exactly what it was.

Fast Times would be Amy's directorial debut. A young girl

from Brooklyn, she was offered the picture after I saw her NYU student film, which distinguished itself by unabashedly dealing with the perils of sex and relationships. But her thick New York accent indicated that she would not have much affinity for casting a West Coast surfer. Her nose oddly puckered, she kept referring to Spicoli as the "soifah boy." Nonetheless, I felt she'd have the guts to put up on the screen the very raw adventures that Cameron Crowe had created. Even though Cameron's legendary script had yet to go before the cameras, we knew that those unmistakable phrases to be uttered by Sean—"Hey bud, let's party." "Awesome, totally awesome!" *"Dude."* "You dick!"—were going to be banging off of mall walls for decades. Universal had the guts to back the play.

Rather than make price an issue, Sean insisted on seeing dailies, a rather precocious request for a new actor. In the past, most actors were barred from seeing the film of what they did the day before. It's a tired practice that has increasingly become passé. Good actors are very smart and are more than capable of determining what they can and cannot see. We were annoyed by Sean's boldness, but we agreed to the request. He also wanted to participate in the casting of his two "buds." Despite the fact that they had so few lines, Sean knew he would be surrounded by them in almost all his scenes. They had to be good actors. Again we were annoyed by his boldness, but we agreed. We cast Eric Stoltz and Anthony Edwards, both unknowns at the time.

Once Sean appeared ready for the role of Spicoli, a new personality had emerged. Drunk and whacked from doing the research of a surfer casualty, Sean was clad at all times in full beach ensemble—all conceived and put together by him—including a long, sun-thrashed wig. He would arrive in the morning with it on and leave without taking it off, presumably to avoid breaking the Spicoli mystique in front of his fellow actors.

Sean's compliant nature during the reading session had long since been replaced by the odd belligerence of a dim "stoner" trying to have a little fun. He managed to sustain this even between scenes, befriending only his surfer buddies in the cast. When Phoebe Cates and Jennifer Jason Leigh tried to ask him some technical questions, Sean in typical Spicoli fashion took the lit cigarette from his mouth, slowly put it out in the palm of his hand, smiled, and walked away. The girls managed to keep their distance for the rest of the shoot. They were the first to wonder if Sean was a "bad boy."

Joe Pesci had a point. We couldn't tell if Sean could act, but we *could* tell he was serious about it. Serious as a heart attack. All of us had the feeling that this guy was not going to go away. The agonizing part is that, after producing a few movies, you become very aware that a film's future is determined by the frail subjectivity of these casting decisions. When the lights go down, audiences don't give a shit about the background, camera angles, or lighting. As important as these things are to the ultimate artistry of the movie, it is the performance that ultimately takes us for the ride. All you are left with is actors acting.

Nothing else.

There should be a sign posted at the entrance to every casting session: "Step forward slowly and at your own peril. A lot of bad things can happen." Because if you think that the rebuffs you have gotten or have yet to get from agents and studio executives are embarrassing and bruising, then you should know that actors are forced to take rejection to a breathless level of pain—particularly when they are beginning their careers. In the whole process of moviemaking, you are about to select and work with a group of people who will get treated (or have already been treated) worse than you.

The stories of rejection are endless. When Dustin Hoffman announced to his family that he wanted to act, even his

Aunt Pearl said to forget it, his looks would kill him. Imagine what the producers were telling him. When Meryl Streep was first auditioning for a part in a Dino De Laurentis film, Dino turned to his associate and said in Italian, "What is she, what is she? She's not beautiful." Unknown to the room, Meryl spoke fluent Italian. Et cetera. Et cetera. Et cetera.

When an actor finally does gain some real power—i.e., becomes a movie star—he or she has amassed a fat bankroll of scar tissue. Stars are seasoned and tough. You can only hope they're not looking to get even. Your ability to work with them, as we shall see, requires diplomacy—a better word may be *respect*. It, too, is part of the process.

Besides the creative aspect of choosing the right actor for the right part, you are responsible for the more mundane task of negotiating a deal that both the studio and the actor's agent can accept. The star of the movie is cast for reasons that involve money as well as ability. Studios are businesses run by businessmen. Rightness for the part is so idiosyncratic that a studio, to make the large investment, will often hedge their bet with an actor who may or may not be as good for the part as a lesser-known up-and-comer. Since they don't really know what actor will create the best artistic choice, they naturally pick the one who is the easiest to sell. The producer and the director have to guide them. This has as much to do with money as it does with smart casting.

I recall being in a preproduction meeting regarding *Ordinary Daylight,* the David Mamet script about an artist who is slowly losing his sight. It was just three days after *The Last of the Mohicans* had opened to a big box-office number. The executive in charge was saying, "Why don't we get Daniel Day-Lewis to play the lead?" I believed this was a fine idea, but no one seemed to remember that when he'd been suggested two months earlier, the response was "Let's not turn this picture into an art-house movie just yet. Let's at least try to get a star!" Does "flavor of the month" ring a bell here? After an $11 million opening weekend, Daniel Day-Lewis's star had risen. The chase for his next picture had begun. In three years he may go back on the "great actor but not a star" list without even knowing it. But for now Hollywood must take a number and wait in line.

When the money says, "Get me one of the actors or actresses on this list or put the script back in the fuckin' drawer," your producer's survival instinct quickly surges through your adrenal glands. You desperately try to find an actor, anybody, the studio thinks they can sell. It's amazing how you can begin to justify the use of a name actor for a role. Any name actor. Suddenly a part written for a Mexican drug dealer turned folk hero fits perfectly for Michael J. Fox. In fact, it becomes a brilliant idea. Offbeat. Unexpected. Maybe it will even provide some comedy.

Without missing a beat, we all become moths to the flame, mercilessly chasing the heat, scavenging after the newest brass ring. It is an essential part of the casting game. Excuse the cynicism, but there is much money at stake. There are guys selling pencils on the Santa Monica Pier who in the name of art took an exasperated chapter from *Network,* jumped on an executive desk, and screamed, "You bastards! If you make me cast that shithead, I'm walking."

Once you have the star or stars of the movie signed up, the remaining casting decisions become more subtle. The studio or financier rarely concern themselves with the subsidiary roles, and the casting process usually continues without much outside interference unless one of the lesser roles becomes too expensive and there is no apparent box-office justification for it.

Here is an inside example of how a negotiation like this occurs:

When Cameron Crowe and I were casting *Singles,* an

ensemble movie with six major parts but no specific lead, we had filled every part but Cliff, the long-haired rock guitarist who drove a flower truck to make ends meet. The studio had consented to make this film without stars because it was going to have a relatively moderate price tag of under $15 million with the expectation of recouping its investment from the "twenty-something" audience for whom they thought it was intended.

We were down to this one last part, and we had seen and/or read everyone in town. No cheap newcomer seemed to have the charisma to pull it off. The budget for the role of Cliff was $50,000. A lot of money if the actor was unknown, but a pittance if ten people outside his immediate family had ever heard of him. It was a pivotal role, and Cameron and I talked about two possibilities: Matt Dillon and Charlie Sheen. We decided that the freshest and most exciting choice was Matt.

It was a good situation. Even though Warner Bros. knew that the casting of Matt would take us over budget, they were interested and understood somewhat his intrinsic value. Matt and his agent, Scott Zimmerman, were also interested. Matt, although very well known, had been in a series of box-office flops. Even *Drugstore Cowboy,* a movie with great quality, ultimately was flat on the balance sheet. Nevertheless, both sides wanted this to work, so you would think that the rest would have been easy.

Matt had a set price of $1 million. This means that in the past Matt had been paid $1 million for a movie. Once a price has been set, the agent uses that as a floor from which to negotiate. The object is to keep getting more for your client, come hell or high water, so there is great reluctance to drop one's set price, because if an exception is made, the next studio negotiation may also ask for a reduction.

Warners had no intention of paying Matt a million dollars for this part. Matt's agent was unwilling to drop his price. The only thing holding this together was that Zimmerman knew that Cameron and I were desperate for Matt, and we knew that Matt wanted to do the role.

There are three arguments a producer can make to try to get a price that has already been set lowered:

- "The guy hasn't been in a hit movie in five years. He doesn't sell three tickets." This is an awkward tactic because not only is it insulting to the actor's agent but it also begs the question of why you want him in the first place.
- "This role will only take four weeks instead of the usual eight. Please give us a discount." The problem here is that future deals won't care how many weeks it took. After all, Marlon Brando didn't cut his "price" when he played Superman's father, even though he only appeared in the first ten minutes of the movie. His inclusion made a difference. More time is not necessarily better time. Even if this approach would be persuasive with someone like Matt's agent, time was not on our side.
- "We'll defer your salary and reimburse you out of net or gross profits," I tried. This is always a hard sell, because even waitresses know that very few people ever see money once the movie is in release, and even if the actor agreed, everyone in town would find out that he'd deferred his salary and would expect him to do so in the future. It didn't fly.

In fact, none of these methods was working. Scott was holding firm, but I noticed that he was getting a little ragged around the edges as the negotiations were becoming imminent. Even though he knew the creative team was supporting

Matt, he could sense—but wasn't sure—that Warner Bros. was expecting a big drop in price. He was calling more frequently, wondering what was going on. After much back and forth, I told the agent that I was having lunch with Terry Semel and I would bring up the matter. Semel is the president/COO of Warner Bros., and for fifteen years, along with the chairman, Bob Daly, has run the most successful film studio in Holly-wood. Known for his shrewdness, he ordinarily would not get mixed up in such a minor negotiation. But, if Terry were caught in a brief moment of weakness—and said yes—Matt would get his money.

This was where the buck stopped. I assured Scott that I would do everything I could. He was encouraged. Aware that Semel liked Matt Dillon, Scott figured that, with some proper begging from the producer, this just might work.

The lunch was held in the private executive dining room, which, disappointingly, offered only two entrées. It was a small room with one small window. There was nothing to do but talk business quickly, get out, and breathe. After several topics were discussed over food served by someone reminiscent of a retired Gestapo guard, I decide to bring up Matt Dillon and *Singles*. Terry politely listened to all the reasons I could muster that Matt Dillon was indispensable to this movie. I realized that while I was airing this laundry list I had eaten all the cookies that the waiter had brought for the two of us. I was forced to chase them with what was left of the Pellegrino.

Terry graciously waited for my final gulp and remarked, "Tell me, Art. What if Matt was crossing Sunset Boulevard today and suddenly got hit by a bus?"

"What?"

"What would you do?"

"You mean, like the bus was moving thirty miles an hour and it hit him flush?" I said.

"Yes."

"Well, I guess . . . I . . . uh."

"Would you still want to make the movie?"

"Well, I guess . . . I . . . uh."

"Exactly."

I returned to my office and relayed this conversation to the agent. Two hours later the deal was closed. The set price dropped $400,000. Matt's brilliant and memorable performance turned out to be quite indispensable indeed.

After the cast has been chosen, the producer's work in dealing with them is far from over. By the time the actors show up for work, their view of you begins to change. The need to kiss your ass is over. They've got the job! They see you standing around the set, and they don't know what the producer does any more than his mother does. They assume you're in charge of schedules and accommodations. Forget about fielding significant questions concerning the purpose of the film or the nature of the actor's role, you are going to get questions like "Do I work this Wednesday?" or "Where's the lunch truck?" I have heard that Joel *(Die Hard)* Silver keeps an entourage on the set specifically to handle these cheap questions, thus avoiding any needless embarrassment and any stripping of that veil of power to which all producers so desperately cling.

Let's face it, whatever trust, hope, and faith actors can muster, they parsimoniously save for the director. Who can blame them? Their faces are about to be blown sixty feet high. It's the director who they think will be guiding their performance. Actors, who are generally vulnerable people before they get a job, come to work even more defenseless. Even the stars, who are as tough as nails, often feel like sitting ducks in front of the camera.

You may become a shoulder to lean on, but only as a last, last resort.

ARE *YOU* TALKING TO *ME!*

The call came about 11:00 P.M., when I was already prepared to give up for the day.

"Well, he's here," De Palma said. "We're going to gather in my room in about five minutes to discuss the script. He's got some questions. You can stop all your moaning. You finally get your chance to meet him. Let's go." He abruptly hung up.

We had fought hard to get Robert De Niro to join this cast. With all the endless negotiations and meetings, I felt that I knew him, that I had already established a bond, an affinity. The fact was, I could do a pretty good imitation of him when I was drunk, but I had never seen or spoken to him.

It was just a few days before *The Untouchables* was to begin shooting, but because of our ability to isolate scenes—shoot sequences out of order—we were able to compress De Niro's shooting time into two weeks and place him at the end of our schedule. This meant that we were not going to get to Bob's scenes for at least three months. I figured that this meeting would be to discuss wardrobe, script changes, and any other loose ends Bob needed before he went off to prepare for the role. He was legendary for obsessing over the smallest detail.

Travis Bickle.

Jake La Motta.

Johnny Boy.

As I got into the elevator, I tried to avoid thinking about how good he was. Even producers can be hopeless fans. I kept reminding myself to remain nonchalant. Let's keep this professional.

Bob was already seated on the couch when I entered. Brian introduced me while Bob stood quietly, eyeing me with the same quiet dismissiveness one would expect him to give a producer whose name drew a total blank. As unimpressed but polite as he seemed to be, I was equally unaffected. Dressed in khaki's, old Top Siders, and a short-sleeved shirt, Bob looked frail and small. He was so unassuming, I thought he might disappear. If De Palma's introduction had not confirmed that this was Robert De Niro, I would've asked for some verification. Perhaps a passport would have helped to explain how this unimposing figure was planning to chill Eliot Ness to the marrow. He didn't look like he could tear paper.

Bob said that he was leaving within the week for Italy, where he planned to eat for the next two months and gain some weight. He wanted to see and try on the wardrobe we'd prepared for Bob Hoskins. He wanted to talk to the prop guy to review the watches, jewelry, cigars, and so on. He was particularly concerned about the schedule. He wanted his workdays to be continuous. All this was done with extreme politeness, always reassuring us that everything seemed really good. He was just checking in, so to speak.

The conversation lasted a few minutes, and then there was a pregnant pause. Bob just sat there without much expression, almost shy. He appeared even thinner. Where was Marty Scorsese when we needed him? I thought. This guy has been defanged. I looked at Brian. Finally, Bob reached into his tote bag and pulled out the script.

"I have a few questions. Maybe I should talk to Mamet," he said, looking only at De Palma.

"Mamet is Art's department," De Palma replied.

Of course. Now I knew why I was sitting in the room. I'd

been assigned the awful task of telling Bob on our first meeting that, after getting several rewrites out of Mamet, I had pumped the well dry. Pushing him any further would be to no avail. De Palma couldn't deal with him, and I had just been sent back to Chicago from Seattle without new pages or even breakfast. But, fuck, this was Bob De Niro. Surely Mamet could take the time to address his concerns.

"I gotta tell you that Mamet has been getting pretty surly."

"Really," Bob answered with interest.

"Personally, I don't think I could get much more out of him. You might have better luck," I said apologetically.

Bob gave me a look that I later learned was one of his "is somebody saying *no* to me" looks. On my first night with him, however, it simply looked like indigestion. I didn't pay much attention to it. He opened the script and started scanning some of his scenes. We waited.

"I've got some questions. You know, some things that I think don't make sense. It's good, it's very good, but I think he needs to explain some things, you know . . . things."

"Well, I agree with that. But I suggest we approach this very carefully," I said.

Actually, I was too embarrassed to tell him the truth, that the gifted rat bastard had made me fly all the way to Seattle, knowing I was in dire straits, only to tell me that it was nice to see me.

"If you want to get something more out of David, I suggest you call him personally."

"Well, if I have to, I guess I can. But I've had some contact with him in the past. He can be difficult. Perhaps you can help," Bob said, finally looking at me.

"Actually, I don't think that will work. It's going to have to come from you."

"Well, if you won't call him . . . ," Bob continued, that Rolaids expression starting to creep back in his eyes.

"I can call him, but it won't be enough. In fact, I don't think if you call him it will be enough."

"Really?" De Palma jumped in. "Have things gotten that bad?"

"Yes," I said. "I don't want to be cavalier, but can I raise the only approach that I believe will work at this stage?" I asked.

Bob nodded.

"Call him and say, 'David, this is Bob. Before we get started I'd like to say that you are a genius . . . and I am shit . . . but I would—"

"I don't think I can do that," Bob interrupted.

"Bob, after what we've been through with this guy, that's the only advice I can give you."

De Palma glanced at me, always eager to enjoy an excruciating real-life drama, and smiled. He had only a few days before he was going to pull the trigger on this movie, and his attention was drifting. With all the endless details that he was trying to button up, he was hoping De Niro's concerns would drift away or at least get tabled until he returned from Italy twenty-five pounds fatter.

Bob took Mamet's phone number, but I knew the call might never get placed. We agreed to meet in the morning and examine the wardrobe. When I returned to my room, I immediately called De Palma.

"Who was that?"

"What do you mean?"

"If you hadn't told me that was De Niro, I'd be sending out an SOS for Hoskins. We bet the farm on this guy. He looked helpless. Hopefully he was just resting."

"He saves it for the dailies." De Palma cackled as he hung up.

The next day it was my as. .ment, as it would be for the producer, to accompany Bob to the production offices and the set so he could review his wardrobe and meet the people he'd be working with.

"Who is this?" Bob said when I called to meet in the lobby.

"Art."

"Art? . . . Art who?"

For a long beat he let me hang there to reconfirm all my self-doubt, then he cracked up. Treating producers like Rodney Dangerfield is a sport that almost everyone in Hollywood would enjoy, but the way Bob laughed at it made me instantly like him.

When we arrived at the set, as inconspicuous as Bob tries to be, everyone working on the movie was aware of his presence. I dropped him off at the wardrobe trailer, where he spent the next two hours meticulously trying on each and every piece of clothing and accessory that was available. De Palma, who was tending to other things, called me over to say that Bob was still in wardrobe and that he wanted to talk to me. When I entered the trailer, Bob was wearing one of the jackets Armani had designed for Hoskins.

He looked at me, smiled, took me aside, and said, "Can I talk to you?"

"Sure," I said. "So, how is everything going?"

"Great, just great."

"So, what do you think about the clothes?"

"Good, very good."

"How good?" I asked.

"Nice. . . . The people here, they are very nice," he said.

"Yeah, they're swell, what about the clothes?"

"I like them, they're good, they're interesting."

"So, let me see if I'm hearing you correctly," I said. "You have given this a lot of thought, and you have come to the conclusion that you hate the wardrobe. You would like me to start over and have it completely redesigned by the time you get back from Italy, under your supervision."

"Exactly."

"Done."

"Done." He smiled.

"Done." I smiled.

Bob is extremely polite, but any producer born with the smallest of antennae would be able to read him. Even though this was going to cost the company another $50,000, I figured, if you get a chance to have Bob De Niro create Al Capone, he must be given every opportunity to do it his way. It makes no sense to commit to Bob and then try to shortchange him.

Bob was happy. He flew to Italy and ate. When he returned three months later, he was totally unrecognizable. Not only had he gained twenty-five pounds but he had shaved the hairline above his temples as well as on top of his forehead to widen his face. It was a strange look. If he'd walked around with a sign on his chest declaring "I am Robert De Niro," people would still have thought he was a contestant for "The Price Is Right." I was starting to worry again. I, like everyone else, had heard that Bob De Niro lives and breathes his role when he's working. He becomes the character until the filming is over. I expected by the time he returned from Italy he would at least have the bearing of a Mafia chieftain, some subtle affectation that said he could kill you without regret. Instead, he had that same meek look as at our first encounter, but this time he was growing bald.

Bob's wardrobe and makeup tests were to be shot in two days. We were in the middle of filming the shoot-out on the train station staircase, so we set up a camera and lights in one of the nearby waiting rooms. I went to the hotel lobby to meet him.

"Bob. It's Art."

"Art? . . . Art who?" He howled. He was really starting to love this.

"I'm in the lobby with a list of my credits."

"Good, I was meaning to talk to you about them." He howled again.

When the elevator door opened, no one in the busy lobby paid any attention. In fact, because of Bob's new look, we had a vast amount of trouble even getting a table in the coffee shop. After several attempts at politeness were spurned by the hostess because she kept eyeing Bob as if he were a shoplifter, she said, "Would you two please stand over there? I'm very busy." It occurred to me that if this was going to happen when people saw his face on the poster, I would be forced to start developing the sequel to *Car Wash*.

Finally, I whispered into the hostess's ear, "Believe it or not, that is Mr. De Niro. Would you please give us a damn table, because we are going to be staying here for the *next three weeks!*"

Three hours after Bob entered the makeup trailer, Brian and I were called away from the set to the area where we were shooting the wardrobe test. De Niro was ready.

For the last three months, almost the entire movie had been shot. We were literally under siege. Paramount was exerting a lot of pressure on us to finish. The good news was that we had already witnessed the bloody killing of Sean Connery, which surprised us as much in dailies as it did in conception. The notion of killing off a movie star was provocative and, as performed by Connery, eventually became an Oscar-winning event.

Connery and I always remained at arm's length. Perhaps I was paying the price for the major run-in that Connery had had years ago with Cubby Broccoli, the producer of the James Bond series. Rumor has it that after the movies had attained massive box-office status, Connery was not compensated from the profits, as he believed he'd been promised. When he demanded more money, Broccoli decided to replace him with Roger Moore. It is called getting cubby-holed. If this is true, it would be easy to understand why Connery's patience for future producers was extremely limited.

Ever since then, when Connery sees a producer he thinks of one thing: his schedule. If he's kept waiting on the set, you get a call. Even in his sixties, with his ham fists, he can kick the shit out of most men, making his moments of displeasure something to keep an eye on. If the set operates like a Swiss watch, you get a Scottish nod. Unfortunately, movie sets never operate like watches. I had to live without any Scottish nods.

A pleasant surprise was watching Kevin Costner emerge as the movie star he later became. When he was cast as Eliot Ness, we were hoping he could pump some life into a thankless "Mr. Nice Guy" role in a movie where all the colorful moves were given to Connery and De Niro. But he did more than that. He gave the role stature. Only when I saw the movie five years later—seeing it as Kevin Costner the movie star playing Ness—did I realize how much of an anchor he was. Despite his daily barrage of questions, Kevin made Brian and me look smart.

Nonetheless, we still had not introduced Al Capone into the picture. No matter what satisfactions we were holding on to, without the soaring presence of the evil protagonist, this gangster opera was not going to work.

After standing around the train station waiting room for an extra half hour, Bob emerged through an old archway near the lockers. The transformation was remarkable. Handsomely dressed in a $3,000 suit—one of ten that were made by an old New York tailor who used to fit Capone—holding a wide-brimmed hat and a partly smoked $25 Havana, he not only looked and felt like Al Capone, for the first time since I'd met him, but he finally looked like Bob De Niro. It wasn't just a matter of putting on some clothes. His entire demeanor was redefined.

It was like witnessing a grand magic trick performed by a maestro. Without uttering a word, by merely strolling to his position in front of the camera, Capone–De Niro suddenly became sly, dangerous, confident, and even witty. The entire crew felt the electricity. There was really no sense in burning any film; the character had been created. Bob just needed to see which wardrobe changes worked the best.

Brian leaned over to me with an "I told you so" grin.

"Well, I guess you and I will be able to work again" was all I could add.

On the ride back to the hotel, after De Niro had returned to his unassuming self, he asked me, "Now, what were those movies you produced?"

THE DIRECTOR

I don't know how God managed, but I'm having a terrible time.

—John Huston on directing *The Bible*

THE FINAL CUT

In 1937 David O. Selznick was lecturing to a film-study group about the functions of the producer in the making of feature films. It was a rather long and tedious speech that went through the process from the script to the release. He talked about working with the costume designers, the art department, the editor, and the writer, but he barely discussed the director, the one guy who says "action" and "cut." Now I don't know what the hell life was like in Hollywood in 1937, but I can guarantee you that the director has to be reckoned with now. In fact, when the movie is being shot and the producer is roaming about the set wearing a colorful scarf for easy identification, pretending to be in control, the guy whose ass he better kiss is sitting in a director's chair looking bewildered, waiting for the setup of his next shot.

Directors come in all packages: good, bad, poised, under-handed, supportive, powerful, and tame. But there is one thread that binds them together. You are about to go into business with a person who can hold on to a level of self-worth that can astonish the most confident of men. Maybe it's a necessary quality to sustain the grueling battle, the physical beating. But show no pity. Understand what it must be like to have tons of equipment, beautiful actors, and fawning assist-ants at your knees, waiting breathlessly for your instructions, twenty-four hours a day. You whistle a melody, and everyone spends the rest of the day trying to remember it. You get to arrive on the set, horsewhip in one hand, megaphone in the other, ready to command the troops. It's the ultimate blow job.

But outside the fleeting power a director gets when he is shooting the movie, the actual work is a bitch. I feel the produ-cer must be as supportive of the director as possible. Perhaps the best satisfaction you can hope for, when it's over, is to know that the picture is somehow better because you were present—even if it is just 5 percent better. It's a private satisfac-tion at best, because if the picture is a hit many other people—not the least of which are the studio executives, clawing for that big year-end bonus—will be standing in line for credit. No one will ever really know if you made a difference except you. You want to be able to look in the mirror and know that, because you were there, the movie was improved. That is your only personal yardstick. Just providing moral support for the direc-tor might make a difference, or a strong hand may be needed. Each situation is different.

Here's the dilemma.

Before the director was attached, the studio looked to the

producer for some leadership in developing the script, budgeting the movie, and gathering the group that would eventually make the thing. Depending upon your relationship with the studio, you occasionally have a voice in determining who will be the director, and your ability to consult and persuade can often influence a choice. But not all studios operate this way. Often the studio, once a script is in satisfactory shape, will quietly (meaning you are not told) slip your script to a director. If he agrees to do it, they will politely shove him down your throat. It is interesting that most producers take this minor slap stoically and then go to Morton's and celebrate. From their point of view, the studio is at least trying to get the movie made, and, hey, who knows, maybe the guy's going to do a good job. The fact that their balls have just been handed to them in Saran Wrap is just another Hollywood annoyance that most of us have been conditioned to handle. For my part, if I can't be on the committee that chooses the director, I'd just as soon work on something else.

Once the director is on board, the power shifts. The studio can't help themselves. If they can, they will avoid the producer and deal directly with the director. I suppose this is not meant as an insult, because the director, once he gets out in some godforsaken location, has the keys to the car, and he can drive the fucker at any speed. One can't blame the studio for perspiring. Inevitably, the producer takes on the role of middleman, squeezed between the guy who says action and the executives who represent the money.

Not all studios bypass the producer, but rumor has it that during filming producers at Disney are handcuffed to the side of the lunch truck, only to be paraded in front of the crew if someone has to be fired. The best strategy I can offer is to maintain a close relationship with your director, so when you are about to be discarded, he will want to back you up. A bond of trust with the director is created when he believes that you can help him make the movie he wants to make. You have to be diplomatic and contributing without impinging on his self-esteem. As production becomes imminent, directors are under assault form all quarters at all times. If the director is smart, he can effectively use you as a buffer and achieve better results.

You also must maintain a relationship with the studio. After all, they are paying you, and they deserve and should get some professional loyalty. The executive in charge of the film must feel that you are at least trying to keep costs to a minimum while fighting for quality. They need you around for more than somebody to blame, and the good executive realizes that.

You have to be tactful, because if the studio senses you're in the director's pocket they will have no choice but to deal with him and circumvent you. It can be a tightrope walk atop the Hollywood sign.

Brian De Palma is a strong test for any producer. He's experienced and tough. He has soared to the top of the hill, but he has also plummeted with extravagant failures. Even though Brian likes to work with producers, to gain his confidence you have to proceed cautiously. When a relationship starts on a movie, you're filled with ideas, but it's best not to offer them all. A producer must pick his spots. I call this my three-out-of-ten theory. If Brian has to endure seven bad ideas, he will not notice the three good ones.

What I did as we began shooting *The Untouchables* was carefully wait at dailies for something that I really felt was critical and then address it. I decided early on that there would be at most five or six times during filming when I could make a contribution by insisting on something and that I would wait for of one of those times before taking a stand.

We were a few days from shooting one of the last sequences in the movie, where Eliot Ness (Kevin Costner) was sitting at his desk recalling the bloody massacre of his mentor, Malone (Sean Connery). It was a private moment. Ness was to open his drawer and pull out Malone's medallion, the one Ness was given while Malone was dying. Ness was to look at the medallion and silently reminisce over a photo of the "untouchables." Ness would then pass the medallion on to Andy Garcia and retire.

Brian wanted to delete the scene. He was concerned about its oversentimentality. He felt it might get laughed at. I felt the sentiment was essential. This may sound self-serving, but I chose this as one of the times to strenuously object. It's important to note that Brian had final cut of the picture, which means that even if he shot the scene he could find a way to drop it. It's also important to know that if you bombard a director with that kind of power with your opinions, you will soon be back in your office. If you carefully pick your spots, you will be heard. De Palma deferred to me and shot the scene. As soon as he did a take, we both knew it would work in a big way. The scene added an unexpected heart that is rarely achieved in a gangster picture.

At the same time, if you earned your stripes, De Palma returned the loyalty. Knowing what he was trying to achieve with *The Untouchables,* that his scope was grander than could be explained to the studio, we were continuously trying to hold the line with the budget. The studio was increasingly frustrated by the rising costs. While I was trying my best to explain to the studio how these additional costs were going to pay off, I was trying to shield Brian from these problems so he could remain focused on the work.

But fears that we were a little out of control persisted. Much of the trouble was the result of the fact that we had been forced to agree to an unrealistic figure before we started. It's odd, but sometimes the strangest expense can light the fuse. A bill for drapes for $40,000 was sent to Dawn Steel's office. Production costs were expanding rapidly, and I couldn't keep my thumb in the cracked dam any longer. Steel, whom Ned Tanen had now designated as the Paramount executive in charge of the movie, was not known for being a wallflower. She's been monthly fodder for *Spy* magazine, which has parodied her outrageous outbursts. I always felt, however, that her bark was bigger than her bite. She mainly smacked around those who couldn't come back and nail her. The best of Dawn was that deep down she really cared about the quality of the movie.

But she was so frustrated by this final cost, she decided to sidestep me and went directly to De Palma. She must have been under a lot of pressure from Ned Tanen, because she was behaving like Captain Queeg. For her it was the final straw. She got Brian on the phone and railed about the damn drapes. We were so deep in the mud that it seemed like a bad joke. We were in Chicago in the middle of winter, trying to complete each day's work on schedule while Dawn was perched on her designer desk, shrieking. There were so many meaningful production problems that affected millions of dollars that the "drape episode" was a misdirected assault. Some unconstructive stand for Dawn to vent her spleen.

When De Palma suggested that Dawn take this insane topic up with the producer, she said, "There is no producer, goddamnit! I am talking to you! From now on you are the producer." Brian hung up and did not return her calls for almost two years. After being told of the conversation, I graciously did Brian's laundry and dishes for the duration of the shoot.

LOST AT SEA

When I started supervising the first draft of *Dick Tracy* for
Paramount Pictures, the writer, Lorenzo Semple, Jr., was on
location in Bora Bora working on *Hurricane*. Since he couldn't
come to Los Angeles, I went to see him. It was a beleaguered
production on a remote location, months over schedule and
millions of dollars over budget. Because there were no television or phone lines installed, the entire company had nothing
to do but sleep with each other. Mia Farrow, knowing the
importance of good lighting, smartly chose the cinematographer. The others were pairing off as best they could. They had
been there for eight months. A raw prison atmosphere was
starting to take over. I had the feeling that many believed they
were not going to leave Bora Bora alive.

After lunch Lorenzo gave me a tour of the sets. They were
in the final preparations for shooting the big hurricane scene,
but neither the special effects machines nor the weather was
cooperating. Things genuinely seemed in disarray. Most
people were talking about the big luau that was planned for the
weekend, but no work was being done.

As we drove up to a large boat, which was cut in half for
production purposes, a man nearby, wearing only khaki
shorts, lay motionless in the sand. His face was positioned
directly in the strong sun; very dark glasses protected his eyes.
His arms were spread-eagled, Christ-like. No one seemed to
bother him as they went about their business. We had to walk
around him to survey the boat and the other sets while Lorenzo
described the vast difficulties in making the film. He told me
that the cast and crew were losing morale daily, that the equipment was breaking down, that the production costs had doubled, that there was no end in sight. The only entertainment

was an occasional magazine flown in from Tahiti. The pressure on the director had been enormous.

As we circled back to our Jeep an hour later, the man was lying face-down, his nose pressed against the sand. He was still spread-eagled, still motionless. Had he not changed positions, I would have assumed he was dead.

"Who is that guy?" I asked.

"Jan Troell."

"That name's familiar. Who is it?"

"The director."

Postscript: When the average filmgoer gets bombarded by a variety of producing credits on the screen, he or she goes limp and thinks of other things. But for those determined to make some sense out of this odd nomenclature, here is another example of how murky a credit can be as it relates to what a producer actually does:

Thirteen years after my trip to Bora Bora, *Dick Tracy* was made at Disney. I ended up with a credit as executive producer because I had been initially attached to the purchasing of the underlying rights from Chester Gould. I sold these rights to Paramount when Michael Eisner and Jeffrey Katzenberg were running the studio. When they moved to Disney, they maintained their interest in the property, bought it from Paramount, and eventually obtained Warren Beatty to star, produce, and direct the cop cartoon. Any work done by Lorenzo Semple was discarded. A new script was developed, and $50 million was spent to make the film.

Through the years my name stayed legally attached to the production, but my body was cut loose. As often happens, input from the past gets quickly dumped. When the movie that I "executive produced" was released, with grand flash and fanfare, I paid seven bucks like everyone else to get my first glimpse of it. *Dick Tracy* had some wonderful moments, but, credit and all, I had yet to meet or speak with the director.

Part III

RELEASE

FOX
Life in the movie business is
like the, is like the beginning
of a new love affair: it's full
of surprises, and you are con-
stantly getting fucked.

—from *Speed-the-Plow* by David Mamet

PREVIEWS

TAMING OF THE SHREWD

The Advil has already worn off. It is three o'clock in the morning, and my heart is palpitating in that dismaying way, when you feel like a time bomb with the fuse lit but you're too embarrassed to mention it to anyone. The bathroom is only half lit from a burnt-out bulb, but I can still see a trace of eczema forming on my right cheek. It's a bad night. While spiraling downward, I am more wide awake than ever. This exasperation is not the result of a bad diet, or a personal loss, or an unpaid gambling debt, or even a failed romance. I merely came back from a preview of a recent movie I produced: *This Boy's Life*.

The preview process is the most tormenting event the producer goes through. For a year or two you supervise the making of a movie. Then, the night of the first preview, just like in school, you get your grade. You are about to receive a series of numbers tabulated from the audience's response to a variety of questions. After untold millions of dollars have been spent, after you have yelled and been yelled at, 350 people recruited from some run-down shopping center in Pasadena join you in the filmmaking process. They are about to become your artistic partner in the reshaping of your movie.

As they wait in line to get in, you can see their faces, drunk with power, knowing that the "numbers" they come up with in most cases will determine the film's commercial fate. They look back at you from their seats. They can tell you are not one of them no matter how casually you try to dress. They can smell the fear.

After careful examination of these numbers, the studio will decide how much to spend on the release of the picture and how many theaters to release it in. Every marketing guy who has done the job for more than six months has an expression permanently chiseled on his face as if primed to say, "Let's not throw good money after bad," while he awaits the results from the preview. Movies are very expensive to produce, and when they are completed, if they do not "open" on the first Friday night, almost the entire investment can be lost. There is an expression on the street when a picture really bombs, "It won't even recover its prints and ads." This means that the studio not only has lost their entire investment in making the picture but also will not recover their marketing costs. I don't have to elaborate. That kind of failure can make executives very ornery.

Since previews provide the first glimpse of how a movie is going to perform, the anxiety level is white-hot on the meter.

If it bombs, a line is formed in the theater lobby, no different from that of a soup kitchen, where the blame is silently poured into each bowl, with the coldest portion saved for the producer. This tap dance can take on the ugliness of a guy in a western bar dodging bullets at his feet.

Such pressure dramatically affects your ability to look at your own movie during the preview. As the lights go down, you no longer can see the film. Instead, you anxiously watch the backs of heads, occasionally coughing or talking or rising to go to the bathroom. Suddenly, when some seventeen-year-old girl with a ripped Alice in Chains T-shirt exposing her see-through black bra ascends and begins moving up the aisle, you panic. You strain to see her expression as she passes, wondering what demographic group she represents. Of course, she represents the MTV cuddly/slut group. My God, that must mean when the movie gets to the theaters, millions of girls will get up and walk out because something caused them to lose interest. You can't help but look again. Was that grimace caused by a weak bladder, or did she think the movie sucked? Is she going to come back? This anguish goes on for the next two hours. Objectivity is out the window.

Before you started shooting, you flirted with the idea of being a patron of the arts, a brilliant contributor to a classy production, a doer of good work. But by the time you get squeezed by the preview process, all you think about is the money.

As the lights return, the audience begins filling out their questionnaires. The dice is tossed. These screenings turn the sturdiest souls into jelly. During our third preview of *The Untouchables* in New York, my dwindling producing career was solidly on the line. It had been three years since I had a picture in release. The last one, *The Wild Life,* was a cheap but hopeless bomb, and there was no way to regard my present circumstances other than to see the release of *The Untouchables* as a desperate comeback attempt. I remember Ned Tanen and I were seated in the large lobby near the refreshment stand with some theater staff and marketing executives. Other than the popping of the popcorn machine and a momentary waft of melody from Ennio Morricone's lush score, the lobby was quiet, interrupted occasionally by the restless patron or, even worse, the dreaded "walkout."

Two thirds of the way through the movie, this sweet elderly lady was slowly heading to the ladies' room for the third time. On her way back, Tanen was unable to control himself. He told me to find out why she wasn't responding to the picture. I balked, but, being outranked, approached her in front of the swinging doors that led back into the theater.

"Was there something wrong with the picture?" I asked.

"Huh?"

"There must be something, was it a little too violent?"

"No, not really," she said. She was trying to maneuver herself around me.

I looked at Tanen and shrugged. He mouthed the words "Ask her again." I moved to the left slightly, blocking her passage.

"Well, hell, we need your help. You can't seem to stay in your seat," I said.

"I quite like it," she said.

"What made you want to see it? Were you a fan of the TV series?" I was out of the gate now; her path was blocked.

"Well, I was invited."

"Recruited?"

"What?"

"How did you get in here?"

"I am Bob De Niro's grandmother."

Embarrassed, I immediately started to scramble out of her

way, attempting to bow courteously at the same time. We ended up doing this ridiculous dance step that happens when two people are trying to get past each other on a sidewalk. She moved to the left, and I, thinking she would move to the right, also moved to the left, and, inevitably, we banged into each other.

"Oh . . . so sorry . . . I . . . uh . . . that guy over there is Mr. Tanen. He made me do this," I said. This time I almost knocked her completely off her feet. As I spun around, she lunged forward into the theater. I careened back into the lobby.

One's own bias often creeps into the analysis of these screenings and can dramatically affect the way a movie is marketed. When we were previewing *Fast Times at Ridgemont High,* it put Universal in a bit of a tailspin. Here was a raunchy high school comedy with an R rating that offended most grown-ups—particularly the grown-ups at Universal who were marketing the picture. At the preview I was sitting three seats to the left and one row behind Bob Rehme, who at the time was president in charge of distribution for Universal. Rehme, a straitlaced and kindly family man, would have a major say in how much money would be spent on advertising and in how many theaters the film would appear. Initially the plan was to open the movie in 1,000 theaters across the country. To support this many theaters, it required a substantial commitment of money for prints and advertising. If you don't believe a movie will work, you open it in fewer theaters, thus reducing your costs.

This was an important screening; Rehme was seeing *Fast Times* for the first time.

The movie started, and as you might expect I was watching Rehme as he was watching the screen. When Spicoli (Sean Penn) turned to his teacher and shouted, "You dick!" Rehme took it stoically, a slight wince but nothing too serious. When

Phoebe Cates was asked during the noon recess, "How much comes out when a guy has an orgasm?" Rehme stiffened and the audience was still. They were too shocked to laugh. When Jennifer Jason Leigh was seduced totally naked in the record time of three seconds by Robert Romanus and he said, "I think I 'came,' " Rehme slowly started to shake his head. I was beginning to sense that this was not going to be his favorite film. By the time Judge Reinhold was caught in his bathroom "jerking off" to a topless vision of Phoebe Cates while still wearing his pirate hat from work, Rehme had turned to stone.

Even though I had the feeling that the audience really enjoyed the movie, they were not as vocal about it as they might have been if it were more conventional. My interpretation of their silence was that they were so stunned they didn't want to miss anything. That as the scenes unfolded, they were riveted.

Marketing executives had another interpretation. They let their own biases affect their analysis, and we were told that we were not going to open the picture nationally as planned. Rehme felt that we should open on the West Coast only and see what happened. This was not what we were hoping to hear. It was another way of saying that no money would be spent on expensive national television ads. Rehme had soured. The preview obviously told him that the movie wasn't going to work, and he was looking to cut his losses.

Well, with luck on our side, the movie opened to huge business on a very limited advertising budget, and the marketing staff had to scramble to get the East Coast theaters to exhibit the picture weeks later, before summer was over. *Fast Times* ended up being one of the most successful high school movies of all time.

The man who has gotten rich by making Hollywood feed off this statistical paranoia is Joe Farrell. Middle-aged, with gray hair and a wolfish grin, Farrell maintains the satisfied look of a man who has come to terms with excessive alimony payments. He has become the ultimate Hollywood bookmaker. In 1978 he formed the National Research Group to assist studios in the market research of their films. Even though the practice of screening movies in front of test audiences had existed for decades, Farrell introduced a modern numerical system of calculating audience reactions, which raised statistics to a new but not necessarily better level. By making the town believe that he had taken the guesswork out of the equation, in my opinion, he has created more havoc and confusion than ever before.

Instead of observing audiences and drawing conclusions instinctively, Farrell provides a simple series of numerical grades tabulated from preview cards.

Although there are several questions asked, the ones used for "scoring" purposes are as follows:

1. What was your reaction to the movie overall? Would you say that it was . . . ("X" ONE)

   Excellent
   Very Good
   Good
   Fair
   Poor

2. Would you recommend this picture to your friends? ("X" ONE)

   Yes, Definitely
   Yes, Probably
   Not Sure
   No, Probably Not
   No, Definitely Not

Once the statistics are compiled, a report is put together, which provides a series of numbers that the studios use to explain to the filmmaker and to themselves what needs to be changed in the movie so the scores will get higher. The assumption is that if the score can increase the movie will be more successful. This assumption has never been proved.

There is a tremendous overreaction to this stuff because a specific number (e.g., 54 percent Definite Recommend means an above-average performance based on the norm of 45 percent) gives the illusion of an exact science. You no longer have to rely on your instincts when watching the previews. You don't have to "feel" the audience anymore. A chart is about to tell you precisely what path to take. Whenever your "gut" is removed from the moviemaking process, everything suffers.

The worst of all is that Farrell's stats are hit and miss at best. Of course, with pictures that are obvious hits or obvious failures, the numbers usually hold up. But those movies don't need numbers. Everyone seeing them can sense the same result. On the pictures that are tough calls and in need of some guidance, my experience is that the analysis is a false crutch laced with double-talk. If these stats are used improperly, you can be wasting your time or even making the movie substantially worse.

Audiences by their basic nature will always feel initially more comfortable with something that they have already seen and liked, and they will mark their cards accordingly. That, however, does not necessarily mean they want to pay seven dollars to get in, three dollars to park, and three dollars for popcorn and a Coke for something that is just like something they have already seen.

Trying to "give them what they want" can be a detestable process. Whatever is fresh or controversial will take time for an audience to accept. You are doomed the minute you start recutting a film solely because the cards preferred one move over another. By reducing the risks you reduce the surprises. You take the "art" out of the equation. Any daring scenes in *Fast Times* would have been destroyed by this process had we not held the line.

The picture can suffer from random changes even if the number goes up. Greater success is very iffy. Taking ten minutes out of a film because several cards say it was a bit too long may have a very minor effect on the number, but the process may gut the movie. An audience's immediate reaction to the shorter version may score a little higher, but as they go home, the film experience may become less substantial and not stay with them. Two days later the film may feel to them like Chinese food—light and forgettable. There is no effort to test for this. If a studio overreacts to these data and insists on making an overrecruited preview audience an equal creative partner, we end up being led by audiences instead of leading them. The end results can backfire.

If you produce movies that take any chances at all—provide any controversy—the likelihood is that they will not preview quite as well statistically as a movie that is more familiar, more derivative, more comfortable. But this does not necessarily mean that the movie will not perform as well once it is released.

With Joe Pesci and Bob De Niro hacking up some guy in a trunk, it was hard to get anyone in the audience to admit that they would recommend *GoodFellas*. In fact, *GoodFellas* previewed horribly. It tested worse than any movie Warners put out that year, and it turned out to be one of Martin Scorsese's most successful films at the box office. The result was rationalized. Those who protect the system simply said that the good reviews changed the audience's mind. But there are an endless number of movies with good reviews—better than those enjoyed by *GoodFellas*—that no one comes to see. The stats simply failed.

Recently, *Hero*, starring Dustin Hoffman, tested very nicely for Columbia. It failed miserably at the box office, but *Single White Female* (without a significant lead actor or successful preview numbers) did exceedingly well for Columbia. Examples like this occur year in and year out. Frankly, for the producer, these examples should be cherished. When the numbers are proved wrong, it inspires executives to take risks, to deviate from the obvious. Without the unexpected hits, the public would only get remakes, sequels, and cartoons.

The Untouchables was about to be released on the same day as *Harry and the Hendersons*. We were told that *Harry* was testing "through the roof." The numbers were unprecedented. Everyone who saw it would definitely recommend it. Nine out of every ten Americans was sure to see it. Aliens would lose their green cards if they were unable to present a ticket stub from *Harry*. Did we dare try to put our movie in the theaters on the same night that this power picture was to open? Paramount, unfazed, wisely held to our date. When *Harry* died a sad but quick death, I asked Joe what happened. He said that the testing only measured how the audience felt when they were in the theater but did not indicate if they'd wanted to see the film in the first place.

This redefines *hustle*.

The difficulty with this research is that no matter what the result, Farrell has an answer to back up his numbers. If the movie fails with good numbers, it was bad reviews that killed it. If the reviews were good, then it was an unsuccessful ad campaign that killed it. If the campaign tested well, then it was the weak cast that killed it, or subject matter that no longer interested the public. The number is always sacred. Maybe the movie just wasn't any good and it took the public a few days to figure that out. The public, in their infinite innocence, passed.

I once asked Joe why we should bother to make the movies and then have them tested. Why didn't we just let the audience read the scripts and test them before we wasted all that money making them? Joe slowly turned toward me and gave me a sidelong look with all his teeth showing. It was like tossing raw meat to Dracula.

But, before we tar and feather Joe, I must say that we are all suckers for the numbers when they go our way.

It took a year and a half to develop and produce the American remake of *La Femme Nikita* for Warner Bros. Even though the movie ultimately belongs to the company that pays for it, when you spend a good chunk of your soul to help it along, you never quite get used to your vulnerable position. Sometimes you can't even name your own baby.

After the movie was completed, we couldn't come up with a satisfactory title. We went through endless lists, from *The Assassin's Heart* to *Sweet Hot Steel*. We settled rather anxiously on *The Specialist*. The customary T-shirts and hats were manufactured. I got used to it. I even started to defend it.

Three months before the movie's release, I get a call from Bruce Berman, head of Motion Picture Productions, saying that they intended to call the movie *Point of No Return*. I shrieked. "*Point of No Return!* How can you come along and call the picture whatever you want at the last minute? Don't I at least get to name the damn thing?"

"I like it," he said.

"You like it! This title is from some awful fucking song by the group Kansas. Can't we get a bit more original than that?"

"Let's just test it," Bruce said calmly.

"What happened to *The Specialist?*"

"We gave it to Steven Seagal for his next picture."

"Unbelievable."

"Let's just test it," Bruce said. I've worked with Bruce since he was a junior executive at Universal, where he helped to shepherd *Fast Times at Ridgmont High.* Through the years he has quietly withstood each frontal and covert assault on his way to head of production. Against this sort of seasoning, I knew I was about to lose this negotiation.

"Oh, tests are bullshit," I said. "C'mon, this is just some last-minute dick waving. Isn't it? This isn't about titles, it's about power."

"Hey, we'll get a number and we'll talk," he said.

"Shit, here we go again." I hung up.

One week later the "one sheet," which is the color poster that you see hanging in theater lobbies and on bus stops, and the movie trailer were shown to select groups in several cities throughout the country with the old title and the new title. Without exception, *Point of No Return* tested much higher than any other choice. So much higher, in fact, that the studio for the first time felt that the marketing would go extremely well. Bruce called with the news. "You have a new title," he said.

"Just like that. . . . Do you know that Bridget Fonda thinks it's so lame that she can't bring herself to say the fucker out loud to the press?"

"The test numbers are great."

"So."

"Really great. I mean, better numbers than we have seen in a long time. Truly great."

"I see."

"Are you listening?"

"Of course. But it's just a test. Just numbers."

"These numbers are so good, it means we are going to *open* your picture."

"Well. . . ." I started to sound like Jack Benny.

"Do you have anything you would like to add?" Bruce asked.

"Yes. . . . I love the new title. . . . Hey, Bruce, when you think about it, *Point of No Return* sort of illustrates the dilemma facing the main character. It lets the audience know she's in a real jam. I think maybe it makes her more vulnerable, more . . . how can I say? . . . winning. It makes the picture feels more personal somehow . . . more . . . more . . ."

You get the idea.

The worst of all of this is that sometimes the stats are correct, and the studio has no alternative but to pay attention and act accordingly. If the numbers are against you, the enthusiasm and the support are simply not the same. We've got to take Farrell seriously because, right or wrong, the statistics affect the momentum of a movie's release—even if it feels like a rectal examination.

As the public (my new partners) filed out of the theater, they seemed rather touched and taken by *This Boy's Life*. They'd even applauded at the end. But when they had to declare if they would recommend it, they chose the Probable Recommend box. Let's face it, this movie did not have a very good preview. I can't get the 37 percent Definite Recommend out of my mind, very aware that it is 7 points under the "norm."

The public had left the theater. Dark clouds were gathering over the empty concession stand as the executives perused the new numbers. I kept mentioning that a lot of people said they would probably recommend the movie. "That's good, isn't it?" I said to anyone who would listen. There were no takers. I was quickly reminded that Joe Farrell says the Probable Recommend box does not count statistically. This is the no-no box. The shit box. If the entire audience would probably recommend the movie, it is of no consequence. Sorry.

So, I guess we are sunk. The director, Michael Caton-

Jones, and I stand together in the lobby, linked as friends and partners ready to take our medicine as the businesspeople file by. They don't use words like *bomb* or *catastrophe*. They politely preface their remarks with "what quality" or "my wife cried" or "sure gets you in the gut," but they inevitably finish with "It's gonna be a tough sell . . . a very, very tough sell."

At home, I finish all my Chinese herbal sleeping pills. They're the stuff you can get over the counter at any good health food store. Acting under the assumption of safety, I am downing in one hour what they recommend as a monthly dose. My courage to swallow stronger stuff has long since gone. I return to bed. Unable to sleep, I quietly listen to a talk radio show discussing the fact that the dispossessed have no safety net, that Palisades Park in Santa Monica is starting to look like Ellis Island at the turn of the century. This is blocks from my house. My neighborhood has become a port of entry for the homeless. One would assume that the effect of preview cards would soon fade when grim reality like this invades the consciousness. For a dedicated movie producer, it doesn't.

Mercifully, within a couple of hours the sun comes up. I trick my body awake by adding a pot of strong coffee to the mix and drive to a 7-Eleven to pick up *Variety*. A small subheadline catches my attention: NEW LINE FILMS TO MAKE *ADVENTURES OF FARTMAN*. The director says, "It will be a *real* comedy with a *beginning, middle and an end*. The *Adventures of Fartman* will revolve around a super hero who becomes Fartman after mistakenly taking a high colonic filled with gasoline."

The news release goes on to speculate that, based on their early testing, the movie starring radio shock jock Howard Stern will have high demographics among young males and could prove very successful at the box office. This news works better for insomnia than any pill. Knowing that there is undeniable truth to this, I am able to sleep for a day and a half. I don't awake refreshed, however, just slightly queasy, trying to keep my resolve for the next phase: *reviews.*

OPENING NIGHT

IT'S NOT MY FAULT

If you're the producer, the first thing you will notice about movie reviews is that your name almost without exception doesn't get mentioned. You have spent months (probably years) getting this idea up on the screen, yet you are never singled out because the reviewers still have no idea what contribution, if any, you have made. You are not alone. Since most critics are failed writers, their envy of screenwriting is so transparent that they rarely if ever give much credit to the screenwriter. It's the director who gets overpraised or unduly villified.

Essentially, you have become the silent partner when the reviews come out. Nonetheless, being charged—even indirectly—for littering America can be daunting, and the criticism can affect you as dramatically as if your name were in lights. There is something about the permanency of print that gets one's attention. Comments on TV or radio can hurt, but they are fleeting. But, when somebody writes in print that everything you have worked for has turned to shit, it feels etched in marble. Set for the ages.

When you began this journey, your concerns were just to get the damn thing made. It is such a long road that you are rarely concerned about the critical reaction until it's your time in the box. Alternatively, when the movie is about to come out, your only concern, other than the ultimate shock of no one showing up, is how is the movie going to be perceived? Is it any good?

There is always the quiet hope that people will regard the movie as something special, even if it doesn't threaten Kevin Costner or Steven Seagal at the box office. The week before the movie is released, you anxiously wait for the bulk of the reviews:

> *Where the Buffalo Roam* is a one-note, highly suspect celebration of gonzo journalist "Dr." Hunter S. Thompson. It slobbers its devotion over a character whose time has passed *before the first scene ends.* . . .
> —*The Village Voice*

> *Car Wash* is the movie equivalent of junk food. It has no more class than a Hostess Twinkie, and it, too, *may make you gag a little.* . . .
> —Pauline Kael, *The New Yorker*

> *Scrooged* is an appallingly unfunny comedy, and a vivid illustration of the fact that money can't buy you laughs. . . .
> —*Variety*

I could go on and on, but why torture either of us? When this happens in large quantities, you immediately call the one person who should know—the executive in charge of the project—to ask how this bloodcurdling diatribe affects the movie. And, more important, your future.

"Don't worry. The kids don't read reviews," he says.

"But, what about me?"

"Well, I . . . could you hold on for a minute? I'm getting a call from upstairs."

"Sure."

A long sixty seconds of silence passes before his secretary returns to the phone.

"Can I have Phil call you in a short while? I'm afraid he's really stuck on this call."

You know by now not to wait by the phone for this return call. You will not hear from Phil again until opening night.

IT STILL HASN'T GOTTEN WEIRD ENOUGH FOR ME

My lawyer Barry Hirsh says, "In Hollywood, the sizzle is always better than the steak." For those of you who need a further explanation, this means that the expectation of a movie before it's released is always higher than the reality of its success or its failure. If you are attempting to negotiate your next deal— assuming you have something else to sell—he recommends you complete this deal before your movie comes out. No matter how high your belief that you are sitting on a hit, you will be at your "hottest" the month before its release.

This is valuable and expensive advice. Barry, who has many high-priced clients, probably makes more money than all of them. Here are the percentages. Fewer than one out of ten movies really make significant money and are perceived as hits.

Fewer than one out of twenty are perceived as good movies. But the oddest phenomenon occurs with a movie weeks before opening night. Endearingly, Hollywood is a town of such optimism and dreams that it gets excited about almost all movies before release. For a short period of time, percentages are thrown out the window and a little bit of grace is shown to those who made the movie. Once the movie opens, unless the results are extraordinary, you hear the same word you hear at the barbershop: *next*.

If you happen to win the lottery and produce a big hit, you don't need a handbook for your next move. Handling success is a breeze. After Ingo Preminger (Otto's less celebrated brother) produced *M*A*S*H,* he took all the money, left town, and was never heard from again. A meaningful option. Although he did this over twenty years ago, it's a move that I have learned to respect. Most producers with a big hit frame two Xerox copies of their first $1 million-plus royalty check—one for the office and one for the home—without the vaguest intention of ever leaving town. After six months of rampant spending, which inevitably includes the traditional accoutrements—a BMW, a minor collection of contemporary California art, some overpriced Navajo baskets and blankets, and architectural plans for the new house from the latest Oriental Pacific Rim whiz—they roll up their sleeves and set up an unmanageable number of development deals, languish daily at some "hot" lunch spot, and hope to get hit by lightning again. It's a good life, but it rarely happens.

What if your car turns the corner toward the theater on opening night and no one is there? That's right, what if your movie is a casualty? You played the game and lost. Desperation fills the veins. Any blind thought that business is going to pick up next weekend is not just wishful thinking, it's a bad fairy tale that *never* comes true.

It's over.

Even if there are some patrons lining up under the marquee when you get out of your car, don't relax, because you'll
probably get the call the next morning from the studio distribution executive explaining in the most matter-of-fact way that
the national numbers are just not there. "But what about that
line I saw at the theater?" He will dryly explain that the line you
saw was just an aberration. It's bad news served cold. It's like
drawing sympathy from a pit boss in Vegas.

It's over.

Or even worse, you discover from friends and family
members that a lot of people came to many theaters in random
cities throughout the country. For an entire weekend, you're
gripped with hope. But on Monday you are told in the same
matter-of-fact voice that according to the dreaded Joe Farrell
exit polls, the audience wasn't comfortable with the movie and
won't be recommending it to their friends for next weekend.
The exit polls sucked.

It's still over.

It's a bomb, and it's time to show what you're made of.

Assuming you won't quit and you don't have a slew of
hits from before this bomb to soften the blow, you will be
facing many hurdles, not the least of which is your credibility.
When I was about to release *Where the Buffalo Roam,* the
movie about Hunter S. Thompson, I was naively feeling a little
"sizzle." Before the official previews, we had a few small
screenings to see how the movie would "play." Hunter usually
arrived with an ice bucket, a bottle of Chivas, and some lem-
ons. I should have tempered my optimism when the only fans
of the movie, who truly seemed to enjoy it, would approach us,
offer congratulations, and then ask if we would like to try some
pharmaceutical ether. This is not a sign that your audience has
a broad base.

During the first preview in San Jose, there was a lot of
laughter. It was an important night, because Ned Tanen was to

see the movie for the first time. I was so naive I thought that if half the people liked it, I was doing well. On the flight back, I was buoyant until I noticed that Tanen chose to sit in the last seat in coach instead of a cushy seat in first class with his junior associates. As I ventured back to the lavatory, Tanen, after seeing me, bent over stiffly and put his head between his legs. His jaw was locked. When I tried to make conversation, he cupped his ears with his hands. It was not the posture of a winner, but I was too drunk to take this as an omen.

The movie was about to come out, and everyone wanted to know what I wanted to do next. I was in the grace period. My calls were getting returned quickly and during working hours. This is a good sign, because if a call gets returned at 1:30 P.M. or after 8:00 P.M. the caller knows you are not there to receive it. The person is being polite, but he really doesn't want to talk to you. Young executives were actually being very deferential to me. Perhaps they were smelling the vague possibility of success—a chance to get in on the ground floor of "hip." Hunter Thompson, Bill Murray, why not? I quickly lined up three meetings to discuss new ideas at three different studios. I was so damn busy that I scheduled these meetings for the week after *Buffalo* was to come out.

Barry was not yet my lawyer. I didn't know about "sizzle."

On opening night the movie imploded. I faced a firing squad without a blindfold. Each meeting was graciously postponed and eventually canceled. I was in Hollywood Hell. For a while I was reluctant to place calls. I felt no news was better than unrequited relationships. When I did place calls, it took days to get them returned—if they ever were. There is nothing more disconcerting than having people come up to you with bullshit concern and ask, "Are you thinking about making another movie soon?" They can't conceal their glee that you have to rethink your place in or out of show business.

Hollywood is afraid of failure. It can't be marketed. Those

connected with it are contagious. The larger lesson here is not only to strike at the right time but also to gain the reassurance that this ostracism is not permanent. My estimate is that it lasts ninety days to six months. The scabs will fall off. Your condition will ease. Within a short time you'll be able to take solace in the fact that you have company. Lots of company. Soon your failure will be on such a long list of failures that its impact will begin to fade. If you are patient and can withstand the rejection, you will soon hear, "Well, at least he got the damn thing made," or "The movie had some nice moments, it was just a hard sell." You can feel when it's time to resurface and show up for that lunch and exude some élan.

I don't want to give false hope. The unwritten rule is "three turkeys and you're out," and many producers before getting to number two are never heard from again.

I have always admired Larry Gordon for walking into a busy Universal commissary for lunch the first Monday after the weekend that *Xanadu* was released. Never one to prefer quality over grosses, Larry had just produced one of the biggest and most unseemly disasters in Universal's history. This film's only redemption was that it had one of the most expensive wrap parties of the year. A lesser man might have been home nursing some wounds, avoiding the whispers, ducking the jackals. I was seated in a banquette near the front entrance when he arrived. His presence caused a bit of a stir. Everybody's adrenaline was racing. The black tower was pitching. For me it was like witnessing a murder and being secretly happy that I'd dodged the bullet. What's that old Hollywood maxim that was stolen from Oscar Wilde? "For true happiness, it's not enough that I succeed, my friends must also fail."

A new, festive atmosphere filled the room. The commissary was vibrating. Yet nothing impeded Larry's command as he strolled slowly to his quality booth in the back, shaking hands with everyone, holding on effortlessly to the full twang of his southern accent. He offered a shit-eating, catlike smile to all present, as if he'd just eaten the big one.

If you are made of that kind of stern stuff, this quarantine evaporates more quickly. You cannot be killed.

For me, it takes a little longer to get out of bed.

LICKING THE ICING

I suppose if you get fortunate enough to pull this job off, you can feel pretty intoxicated. It is essential to bear in mind that you get to make large sums of money off the backs of some very talented people. You even get to share credit—and some producers can do this with a straight face—for making vast creative contributions to the finished film. The best part is you get these accolades whether you want them or not. The making of a quality movie and/or hit is such a rare and unpredictable event that the community has no choice but to parade the participants and tar and feather the victims.

For me, the magic is in the making of the movies. The final outcome is relevant only in that it directly affects your ability to get money to continue. John Huston said, "The experience of making a movie is better and more important than the film itself." The true joy is in the doing. The producer, if he has followed the rules, gets a ringside seat in the most exotic locales, to squabble with, observe, aid, and embrace some of the most gifted artisans around the world.

The downside, of course, is living with the constant impending doom of failure. As time goes on, fending off the horror of losing becomes more significant than getting success. The painful admission is that if you aren't careful, you start to produce defensively. You begin to behave like the very studio execs you complain about. Not taking chances becomes your swan song. Inevitably, as time marches on, you find yourself responding to menopausal ideas with red-faced excitement.

Once you have gotten your money, you begin to answer to gentler, safer concepts. Usually these are of the midlife crisis variety, where an old man who really still has "what it takes" picks up that twenty-year-old girl in his new Ferrari and does what you know he can still do. Redford and Beatty are flirting with this stuff daily. Even sillier are those limp angel movie ideas, where bad people, if they become very, very good, get second chances.

You get the drift.

Hollywood quickly loses its patience as it turns to sweeter blood.

I can hear the footsteps. I have already started to darken my beard. Gray is not one of Hollywood's favorite colors. Let's face it, could there be anything more sorry than an aging, ashen-faced producer standing outside a reception office with a glistening forehead, waiting to see some new Versace-clad key-chain swinger, hoping to sell him his wares? There may as well be a banner draped across Sunset Boulevard between Tower Records and Book Soup that reads: WELCOME. WE CELEBRATE THE LATEST, THE FRESH, THE UNBORN. In fact, as you read this, there are busloads of new people arriving, bubbling with movie ideas, sated with mediocre film school educations, punished by years of watching MTV, just waiting to rape, pillage, and taunt an industry that is already burdened by taking itself way too seriously.

Nevertheless, with a little luck there can be a bright side to all this producing stuff. As you boldly weave through the Hollywood roadblocks, building relationships and learning the talk, you may stir up some surprising results. In a town where cynicism is a breakfast food and competition is severe, you just may make a difference. You just may be the one . . . the one to bring something rare and noteworthy to the screen.